HELPFUL HINTS FOR

# ENJOYING COIN COLLECTING

# HELPFUL HINTS FOR
# ENJOYING COIN COLLECTING

Second Edition

Bill Fivaz with David C. Crenshaw

Metropolitan Coin Club
of Atlanta, Inc.

Helpful Hints for Enjoying Coin Collecting

Written by Bill Fivaz with David C. Crenshaw

Edited by Peyton M. Smith

Cover Design by Lianna Spurrier

Published by Metropolitan Coin Club of Atlanta, Inc.



Published in the United States of America

Second Edition

Library of Congress Control Number: 2026902650

Lulu Press, Inc.

Morrisville, North Carolina

ISBN: 979-8-218-91867-5 (paperback)

This book is dedicated to my late wife, Marilyn, my best friend and companion for 69 years. I couldn't begin to thank her enough for all the time she spent alone over the years as the result of my 36-plus years on the road with Nestlé and all the years in pursuit of my hobby.

She was truly "one of a kind"—loving, understanding, and resilient, even after all those coin show weekends, Summer Seminars (which always fell during our wedding anniversary), and hours spent in my "coin office" at home. Her support and indulgence over the years that enabled me to spend time with my hobby did not go unappreciated.

Thank you, honey.

# Table of Contents

Foreword . . . . . . . . . . . . . . . . . . . . . . . . . . . . . . . . . . . . ix

Preface . . . . . . . . . . . . . . . . . . . . . . . . . . . . . . . . . . . . . xi

Introduction . . . . . . . . . . . . . . . . . . . . . . . . . . . . . . . . . . xiii

Acknowledgements . . . . . . . . . . . . . . . . . . . . . . . . . . . . . xv

1. The Key to Success:

   Arm Yourself with Numismatic Knowledge . . . . . . . . . . . . . . . . 3

2. The DOs and DON'Ts of Coin Collecting . . . . . . . . . . . . . . . . 5

3. Coin Cleaning Basics . . . . . . . . . . . . . . . . . . . . . . . . . . 13

4. Safe and Simple Coin Storage . . . . . . . . . . . . . . . . . . . . . 17

5. Converging on a Convention . . . . . . . . . . . . . . . . . . . . . . 21

6. Buying Coins Through the Mail . . . . . . . . . . . . . . . . . . . . 25

7. Bidding at an Auction . . . . . . . . . . . . . . . . . . . . . . . . . 29

8. Tips on Mailing Coins . . . . . . . . . . . . . . . . . . . . . . . . . 33

9. Grading Hints . . . . . . . . . . . . . . . . . . . . . . . . . . . . . . 37

   Grading Hints for the Indian Cent (1859–1909) . . . . . . . . . . . . . 41

   Grading Hints for the Lincoln Cent (1909–2025) . . . . . . . . . . . . 44

   Grading Hints for the Buffalo Nickel (1913–1938) . . . . . . . . . . . 46

   Grading Hints for the Jefferson Nickel (1938–present) . . . . . . . 49

   Grading Hints for the Mercury Dime (1916–1945) . . . . . . . . . . . 52

   Grading Hints for the Roosevelt Dime (1946–present) . . . . . . . 55

   Grading Hints for the Standing Liberty Quarter (1916–1930) . . 57

   Grading Hints for the Washington Quarter (1932–2025) . . . . . . 59

   Grading Hints for the Walking Liberty Half Dollar (1916–1947) . . 61

   Grading Hints for the Franklin Half Dollar (1948–1963) . . . . . . 63

   Grading Hints for the Kennedy Half Dollar (1964–present) . . . . 65

Grading Hints for the Morgan Dollar (1878–1921)............66
Grading Hints for the Peace Dollar (1921–1935).............67
10. Understanding AU-58 and the Nuances of Coin Grading......69
AU-58: The Grade of the Future? ........................72
Almost Unlimited Bargains in AU ........................75
It's Confession and Revelation Time!......................78
11. Weak Strike Information.............................81
12. The Modern Minting Process ............................91
13. Numismatic Terms and Definitions
General Numismatic Terms ............................95
Bourse Floor Jargon ..................................100
Acronyms and Companies ...........................103
14. Recommended Reading for Collecting US Coins............107
15. Why Not Join a Specialty Club? .........................111
16. 10 Rules of Thumb for Coin Collecting...................117
17. 25-Question Coin Quiz.................................119
25-Question Coin Quiz Answers.........................122
Index ...............................................123
About the Authors.......................................126

# Foreword

## To the First Edition (1999)

When Bill Fivaz does something, he does it enthusiastically, correctly, and in a way that everyone appreciates. The book you now hold is no exception. Here is a guide meant to be *used*—certainly if you are new to numismatics, but also if you've been at the game for a long time. I enjoyed looking through it, and along the way I picked up some pointers that I had either forgotten or never known.

In today's world we are all in a hurry. We want instant information, instant gratification, instant everything.

All too often this leads to unfortunate results. In the hobby of rare coins, it simply is not possible to learn everything all at once, or even in a short time.

However, if time is precious to you, this book by Bill Fivaz will make good use of it! In the following pages Bill distills a tremendous amount of knowledge in succinct chapters. Skim through it quickly or read it carefully from beginning to end. Either way, there is a lot at your fingertips.

Today the world of coins and coin collecting is large and complex. However, one need not be daunted with the prospect, as *Helpful Hints for Enjoying Coin Collecting* is the numismatic equivalent of Rand McNally's popular *United States Road Atlas*. Users of the atlas might never visit all of the towns and counties in America, but an hour spent with it will give a general guide to where everything is and how everything ties together. So it is with this book. An hour or two spent looking through it will put you on the highway to where you want to go—and may well point you toward an interest and specialty in Morgan dollars or Standing Liberty quarters or some other area.

Importantly, Bill is not trying to sell you anything or influence you in your coin-collecting journey (although he does have a personal predilection for error-type coins and interesting die varieties). Rather, he generously shares information he has gathered over many years on many subjects. The term "unbiased" is certainly appropriate. The purchase and collecting decision are yours to make. Bill simply shows you what's available, and in a masterful way.

This book has been needed for a long time. Here it is. Congratulations, Bill, on a job well done.

Sincerely,
Q. David Bowers

# Preface

When Bill Fivaz first asked me (well, more like "strongly encouraged" me) to help bring *Helpful Hints for Enjoying Coin Collecting* into the 2020s, I didn't hesitate for a second. Truth is, I've been connected with Bill and his work for more than half a century. I first did business with him by mail in 1973—I was a 15-year-old running my own little mail-order operation, "Nobody's Perfect," which specialized in error coins and varieties. Four years later, at the 1977 ANA World's Fair of Money in Atlanta, I finally met him in person. I sat in on a seminar he was giving about errors and listened to him talk about the famous 1937-D 3-legged Buffalo nickel. When he asked the room if anyone knew how the missing leg happened, my hand shot up—*I* knew it was caused by an overzealous Denver Mint worker, who polished away the bison's front leg while trying to remove clash marks. Bill grinned, pointed at me, and said, "I'm not calling on David—he already knows everything about errors!" The room laughed, and from that moment on we've been friends, co-conspirators in the errors and varieties world, and occasional sparring partners over grading nuances (especially AU-58 coins).

I've also been a devoted reader of *Helpful Hints* since the 1999 edition landed on my desk when I was 41 and already deep into collecting, but its pages full of Bill's friendly, club-meeting voice still taught me more practical lessons than any pricing guide ever could.

Now, after countless bourse-floor conversations, late-night grading debates, and a few friendly arguments over those same AU-58 coins, the idea of co-authoring an update with the man himself feels like the honor of a lifetime.

My job was straightforward on paper—drag a beloved 1999 classic into 2026 without losing its soul. In practice, that meant rewriting or heavily expanding almost every chapter so that the advice actually matches the world we live in today: evaluating high-resolution images on our phones, instant submissions, marketplace apps, PVC-free flips, and a grading landscape that has evolved dramatically. Among the updates, you'll notice right away that

- "Cleaning of Coins" is now "Coin Cleaning Basics," with far more emphasis on what *not* to do.
- "Storage of Coins" became "Safe and Simple Coin Storage" and reflects modern holders and materials.
- "The Minting Operation" is now "The Modern Minting Process," with fresh explanations of current US Mint technology.
- The old "Buying Coins Through the Mail" and "Tips on Mailing Coins" chapters have been expanded and brought into the age of package tracking and insured shipments.
- "Recommended Reading" is now "Recommended Reading for Collecting US Coins," categorized first by general topics and followed by books from the broader numismatic literature on specific series and subjects.
- "Why Not Join a Specialty Club?" is now structured topically and includes clubs' web addresses or social media accounts.

The biggest addition, though, is a brand-new chapter I wrote titled "Understanding AU-58 and the Nuances of Coin Grading." Ever since Bill's groundbreaking 1986 article, "Is AU-58 the Grade of the Future?" in *The Numismatist,* he has championed the idea that top-end About Uncirculated coins—especially AU-58s—offer eye appeal and value that often eclipse lower Mint State pieces. In the quarter-century since, he's followed up with "Almost Unlimited Bargains in AU" (2013) and "It's Confession and Revelation Time!" (2020). I've taken those three cornerstone articles, brought them together with new photographs and current market observations, and created (what I hope is) the definitive modern discussion of why AU-58 remains one of the sweetest spots in today's market.

Long-time owners of the 1999 edition or the 2004 reprint will still find their favorite stories—Bill refused to let me cut certain classics—but virtually every page has been refreshed, fact-checked against the realities of 2026.

If you're a brand-new collector looking at a coin at arms-length with your loupe during your first club meeting, this book is written for you. If you're a veteran who argued with Bill in 1999 about whether an AU-58 could ever be "better" than an MS-62, this book is also for you. Either way, be prepared to smile, nod, and pick up a new trick or two.

My goal was simple: keep Bill's warm, over-the-table-at-the-club-meeting tone while making sure every piece of advice is accurate and useful in 2026 and beyond. I think we got there—though Bill and I did have a few very minor disagreements along the way. (Old friends are allowed.)

Enjoy the book, cherish the coins, and keep asking questions. This hobby is still as welcoming as ever, and there's always room for one more enthusiastic collector at the table.

David C. Crenshaw, 2026

# Introduction

A couple of months ago I was at a meeting of the Metropolitan Coin Club of Atlanta, and I spotted a brand-new member—maybe 25 years old—who was clearly hooked on coins already but didn't yet know how to look through a loupe. He was holding coins improperly but asking terrific questions and soaking up every answer like a sponge. Watching him reminded me so much of another young man I saw almost 30 years ago, the one who started me down the path to writing *Helpful Hints for Enjoying Coin Collecting* in the first place.

When I wrote the original *Helpful Hints* back in 1998/99, the internet was still dial-up, eBay was brand-new, NGC and PCGS were still fighting for market share, and most of us were still mailing coins in 2"×2" flips and paying with paper checks. A lot has changed! Today that same enthusiastic beginner is just as likely to be buying raw coins on Instagram and submitting them through a drop-off point in five minutes or studying die markers on a 4K monitor using a $79 digital microscope.

The little three-ring binder I handed out at club meetings in the 1990s turned into the 1999 book you may have on your shelf right now, with a second printing in 2004. Both printings sold out years ago, and for a long time I thought, "Well, that was fun, but it's done." Except the questions never stopped. I still get emails and phone calls asking where somebody can find a copy or whether certain advice from 1999 still applies in 2026.

So here we are with an updated and expanded edition, thoroughly revised, redesigned, and enriched with new material. My good friend and fellow error/variety nut David Crenshaw didn't hesitate for a second to let him take the lead on this update. He has redone huge sections, brought in gorgeous new photographs, added chapters on today's tools and pitfalls, and generally dragged the book into the 21st century, while somehow keeping the same "club meeting" tone I've always tried to use. I reviewed every page, mildly argued over a few things (as old friends do), and I'm proud to have both our names on this edition.

If you're completely new to collecting, this book is for you.

If you bought the 1999 or 2004 version, you'll find plenty that's fresh (but also a few favorite stories I just couldn't bear to cut).

If you're an old-timer like me, maybe you'll still pick up a trick or two—I know I did while we were working on it.

Coin collecting remains one of the most welcoming hobbies on earth. New people join our ranks every single day, and my hope is that this updated edition will help them get started on the right foot, avoid some expensive mistakes, and fall in love with the hobby the same way we all did.

Enjoy the journey, handle your coins with care, and I'll see you at the next club meeting.

Bill Fivaz
2026

# Acknowledgements

## To the First Edition (1999)

In a book such as this, although one person's name is listed as the author, it would be more accurate to include all those dedicated and knowledgeable people who, in one way or another, made important contributions to the finished work.

I would like to thank the following numismatists who took time out of their busy schedules to provide their expertise and encouragement in so many areas:

**Bill Atkinson**—The consummate numismatic consumer advocate. Bill has long been dedicated to the advancement of numismatics through his insightful articles in *Coin World* and other trade publications. He tells it like it is, and his excellent writing style offers solid recommendations and warnings to collectors at every level for how to derive more personal enjoyment from the hobby. Bill reviewed the proofs of this book and made many excellent suggestions for improvement.

**Q. David Bowers**—What accolades have not been written about this most prolific author and numismatist? Winner of virtually every award and honor in the hobby, Dave provided the impetus to make this book a reality. In 1998 I sent a rough copy of the manuscript—originally expected to be merely a guide used within our local coin club for new members—hoping to obtain permission to include one article from his "The Joy of Collecting" column published in *Coin World.* After reviewing it, Dave encouraged me to make it available to a larger market as a book. His suggestions and review of this work are greatly appreciated.

**Ken Bressett**—Another close friend, whose expertise and input I deeply respect. As with Dave Bowers, Ken's accomplishments are well known and his excellent suggestions in the formation of this book are very much appreciated. He also reviewed the proofs and did a great deal of polishing to make it more reader-friendly.

**Randy Campbell**—A third-party grader/authenticator who updated the sections on Morgan and Peace dollars in the "Weak Strike Information" chapter of the book. Randy's knowledge in this area is well known and respected by the numismatic community.

**J.P. Martin**—Formerly the leading numismatist at ANAAB for the American Numismatic Association in Colorado Springs and now one of the owners of the Independent Coin Grading Co. (ICG) in Englewood, J.P. is responsible for several of the chapters in this book. It was my pleasure to assist J.P. in many grading and counterfeit-detection seminars over the years, and I never left the seminar without more appreciation of his expertise in all areas of numismatics.

**J.T. "Bubba" Stanton**—A constant source of encouragement and knowledge, Bubba has guided me along every step of bringing this book to you. His close friendship is a treasure, and his many valuable suggestions have truly transformed this book from a rag-tag effort into something I feel can be a solid benefit to the coin collector.

**James Taylor**—Former Director of Education at the ANA in Colorado Springs, James is currently also an owner of the independent third-party grading service ICG in Englewood, Colorado. He has been a role model for me in his efforts to educate the public in numismatics in as many ways as possible. His encouragement and friendship over the years has been a positive influence in my efforts, including this book.

**Fred Weinberg**—A well respected West Coast dealer and all-around good guy who, like Randy, updated the gold section in the chapter on weak strikes. Fred's expertise in this area is outstanding, and I thank him for his contribution to this work.

## To the Second Edition (2026)

A lot of years have passed since the lines above were written. Some of the fine folks I thanked in 1999 are no longer with us, others have retired, and the hobby itself looks very different. I'm grateful to every one of them for helping a little club handout become a real book.

For this updated and expanded edition, I especially want to thank my good friend **David Crenshaw**, who took on the heavy lifting—rewriting large sections, commissioning new photography, modernizing the layout, and shepherding the manuscript through a new copyeditor and publisher. He kept after me until it was finished, and the book is immensely better for his effort. Whatever new collectors learn from these pages in the years ahead will be largely due to his talent and persistence.

Thank you, David. It's been a genuine pleasure.

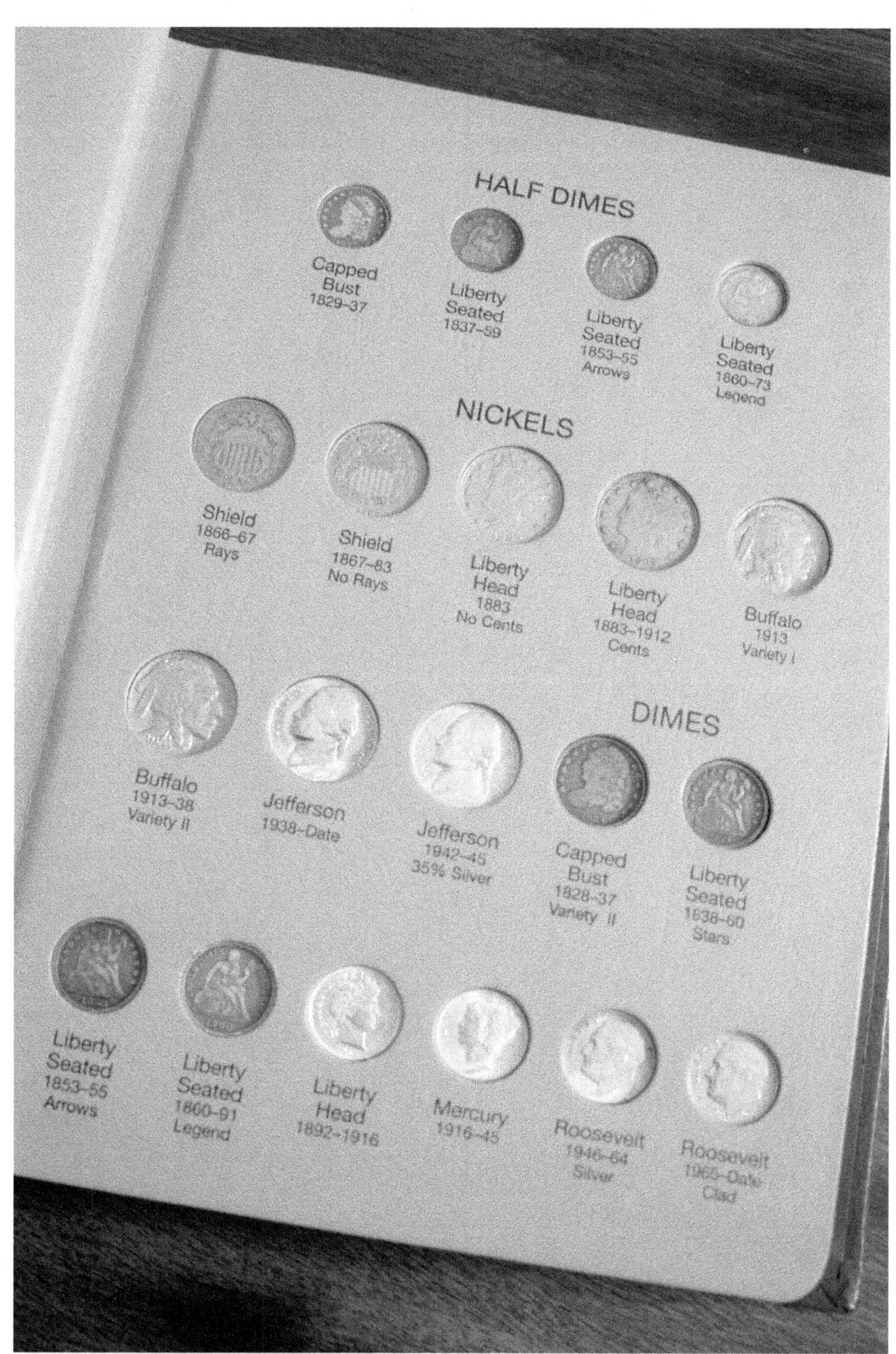

(Courtesy Lianna Spurrier)

# The Key to Success:

## Arm Yourself with Numismatic Knowledge

by Q. David Bowers

The key to being a successful coin buyer, to make advantageous purchases in the market, is summed up in one word: knowledge.

Two weeks ago, I included these quotations in my column:

Confucius said, "The more you learn, the better luck you will have."

George Santayana said (paraphrased), "Those who cannot remember the lessons of the past are condemned to repeat its mistakes."

Here is a little formula that will spell success—as well as enjoyment—for you:

1. Read as much as you can. There is no better way to gain knowledge than to buy books and read them. For a few hundred dollars, your favorite rare coin dealer can sell you an armload of worthwhile books, or you can buy books by mail. Emphasize books that tell about numismatics and coin history (investment books could be fine but should be purchased only after you have a basic library on numismatics and history).
2. Study market trends. In particular, concentrate on items that are *not* "hot." Review the dozens of different niches in American numismatics to see which one(s) would be interesting to collect. If there is a club or group in this niche, sign up as a member.
3. Buy slowly at first, and increase your collection as you gain knowledge.
4. Emphasize quality first and price second.
5. Form a collection, not an "investment accumulation."
6. Buy what you think is worth buying, not what someone else wants to sell you. This will give you a high level of comfort when you review your purchases.
7. Most important: You only live once. Coins are not a necessity of life. No one has to buy coins. Thus, it is important for you to *enjoy* coins.

Consider numismatics to be a center of pleasure, of enjoyment, of happiness in your life. If you have a dispute, settle it quickly. If you encounter someone or something you don't like, walk.

You are in charge of your future.

(From *Coin World*, August 1998. Used with permission of Q. David Bowers.)

# The DOs and DON'Ts of Coin Collecting

The following is presented primarily to help beginning numismatists understand a few of the basic dos and don'ts of coin collecting. However, new and old collectors alike would benefit from this review. I hope that the pointers given here will lessen the possibility of harming a coin through improper handling, storing, and cleaning, and at the same time enhance your enjoyment of the hobby.

## The Task at Hand

Probably more collectible coins have been ruined over the years by improper handling than by any other cause. Needless to say, there is a right way and a wrong way to hold a coin.

Coins should always be held between the thumb and index finger, with those two fingers touching only the edge of the coin. Never touch the obverse or reverse surfaces. Your skin contains a certain amount of oil; touching these surfaces leaves behind fingerprints that can ruin a coin in a relatively short time. There's no way to remove unsightly fingerprints without being able to tell that the coin has been cleaned, so it's a good idea to get into the habit of holding a coin properly at all times—even one that is well circulated.

Fingerprints can ruin a coin in a relatively short period of time. Unfortunately, they cannot be removed without leaving signs of cleaning. (Courtesy Chet Hogan)

Additionally, always make sure your hands are completely dry and clean. In some instances, particularly if you have exceptionally moist hands or if you are examining a Proof coin, cotton gloves should be worn for extra protection. These can be purchased very cheaply online or from your local drugstore. Don't wolf down something like a chicken salad sandwich or snack on potato chips while looking

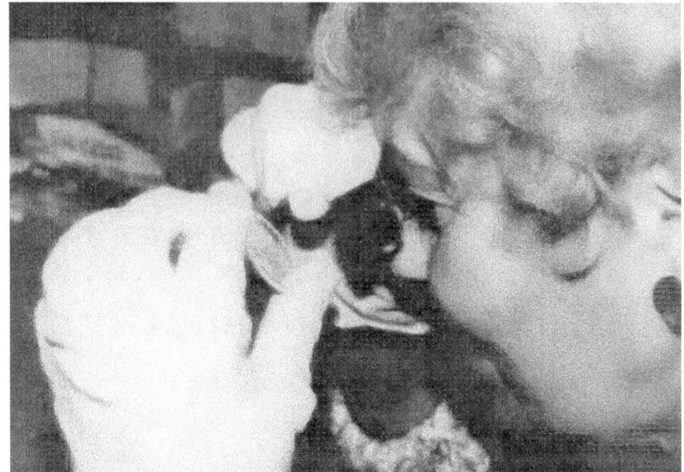

(Left) Always make sure your hands are dry and clean before you handle a coin. If you have exceptionally moist hands or if you are examining a Proof coin, cotton gloves should be worn for extra protection.

(Below) Be sure to turn your head when you sneeze or cough and wait a few seconds before going back to examine the coin.

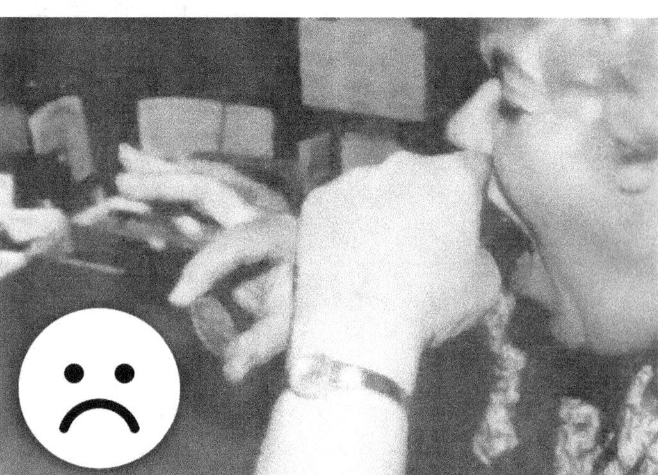

at coins. If you do, you'll be sorry later. Perhaps avoid food all together while handling coins.

As a collector, I encourage you to talk about your coins, but please don't talk *over* them. Tiny droplets of saliva often are expelled when you speak and later may show up on a coin as spots that are difficult (if not impossible) to remove. Similarly, don't forget to turn your head when you sneeze or cough, and wait a few seconds before turning back to examine the coin.

Be especially respectful when examining other people's coins.

Finally, it's very important to hold the coin you're examining over a soft surface (a folded towel will do in a pinch) so that, if you drop it, the coin will be somewhat protected.

## Shedding Light on Coin Examination

Of vital importance—once you've learned how to *hold* a coin—is knowing how to look at it. I highly recommend that you first study a coin with your naked eye to gain an overall impression before using a magnifying glass or loupe. If the coin doesn't make a good first impression, chances are it won't look any better under a magnifier!

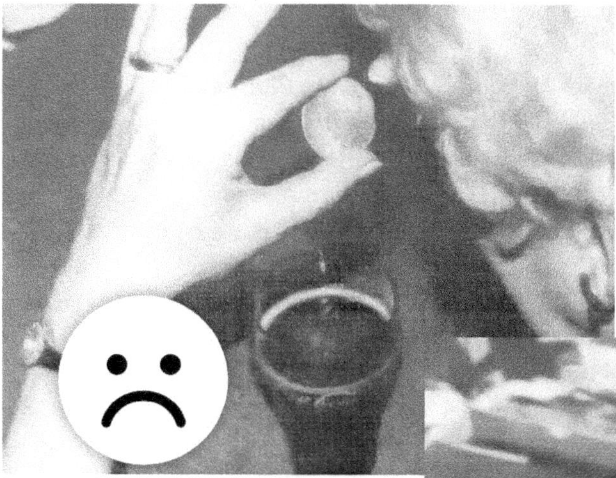

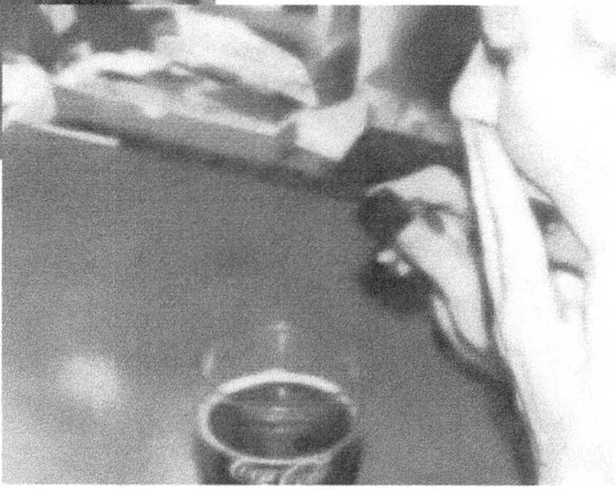

Don't eat or drink when examining coins. You could be sorry.

A popular magnifier is the Hastings Triplet, a loupe made by Bausch & Lomb. This magnifier has precision-ground lenses and little or no distortion at the outer edge. Though somewhat expensive, it is well worth the investment in the long run. The recommended magnification for grading is 5× to 7× (preferably the latter). Anything higher than this is overkill, as you simply can't see enough of the coin's surface at one time to grade properly. Error and variety collectors, though, sometimes prefer a higher magnification than that recommended for grading, frequently using a 10× or 16× glass.

When looking through a magnifier, hold the glass near your eye at a comfortable distance and bring the coin toward you until it comes into focus. Keep both eyes open for easier focusing. If you hold the glass close to the coin at a distance from your eye, you narrow your field of vision dramatically and limit your ability to observe important features on the coin.

Proper lighting is also very important when studying a coin. The ideal light sources are a 100-watt, incandescent bulb situated about three feet from the coin, or a 50-watt bulb from about one foot away. If those bulbs are unavailable, warm white or natural daylight LED lamps are the best modern replacement to show clear color and enhance contrast. Many collectors use a small, high-intensity lamp. Avoid standard low-CRI LEDs, fluorescent lighting, and the ultra-bright overhead lights found

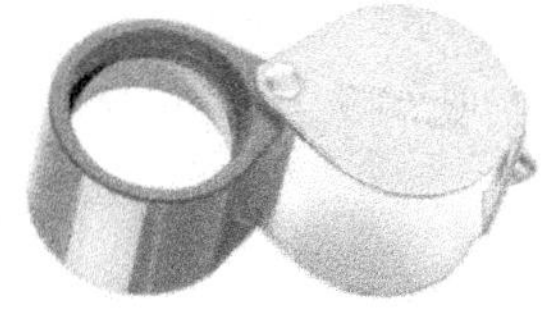

The Hastings Triplet magnifier has precision-ground lenses and little or no edge distortion.

in some jewelry shops whenever possible, as they can add a false impression of brilliance to many coins.

Rotate and tip the coin (the so-called "tip-n-turn" method) so that light reflects from as many angles as possible. On a high-grade specimen, first determine whether or not it is Uncirculated by closely examining the first points of wear. Wear often is first signaled by telltale color differences on high points of the coin's relief. Prepare ahead of time by learning these areas and the striking characteristics of each series you intend to collect. This is important—you must know *where* to look on a coin as well as *how* to look at it. And don't forget to look at the third side of every coin: the edge.

Sometimes a good stereo microscope can be helpful, especially if you are trying to determine if the lines on the surface of a coin are raised (such as from die polishing) or incuse (such as hairlines or scratches). A stereo microscope can also be valuable when checking for alterations, such as added mintmarks, or confirming diagnostics of genuine specimens.

Remember, sight is a faculty, but *seeing* is an art.

## Cleaner Isn't Better

Many of you have asked at one time or another, "Should I clean my coins?" The best advice is, *don't!* Innumerable coins have been ruined by "cleaning" with the intention of improving their appearance.

Collectors have attempted to clean coins by almost every means imaginable (and some you wouldn't believe): pencil erasers, toothpaste, steel wool pads, copper cleaners, and chlorine bleach, to name but a few. For silver coins in particular, the most popular cleaning method is "dipping," or submerging a coin in a chemical solution and then rinsing it. Although dipping sometimes improves the overall appearance of a coin, it's easy to over-dip and destroy the original luster of a piece.

If you see a coin that shines like the front bumper of a '57 Chevy, chances are it's OD-ed, "over-dipped." Overdipping results in a coin that looks lifeless and washed out, totally devoid of its original luster. It is important to remember that any dip is a form of acid, and the process of dipping strips away some of the coin's surface metal each time.

**Although dipping sometimes improves the overall appearance of a coin, it's easy to over-dip and destroy the original luster of a piece.**

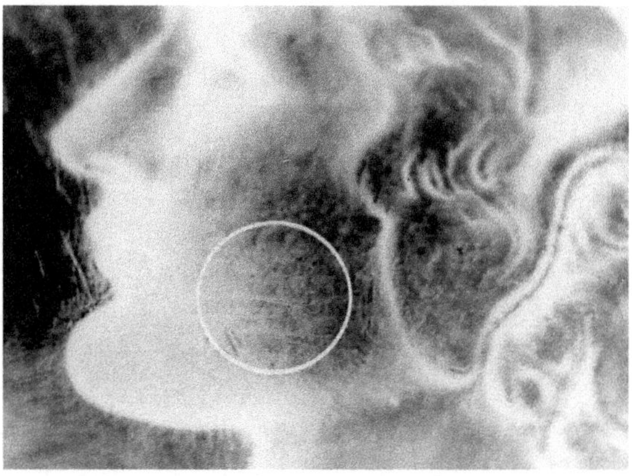
The scratches on this coin resulted when it was slid into and out of an album with acetate "slides" covering the front and back of the coin.

Of course, there are many coins that you shouldn't even think about dipping. Some commercial solvents that have a good track record for silver coins will discolor copper or nickel pieces. If you *must* clean gold coins, probably the safest method is to use mild soap and warm water. Be sure to pat dry the coin carefully and completely. Hairline scratches can result from improper drying, especially on Proof coins. Use a soft cloth or towel and pat them dry—don't rub.

For more information about how to clean coins safely, see Chapter 3, "Coin Cleaning Basics."

## Housing Your Coins

Once you've invested some money in your collection, you'll want to preserve it as best you can.

Various types of albums have long been available for storing your coins. The first were the Whitman coin boards introduced in the late 1930s, followed by the familiar blue Whitman folders, which most of us probably used during our first years of collecting. These albums, though, offer little protection for the exposed obverse of the coins.

Later, albums with acetate "slides" covering the front and back of the coin openings were marketed. These, however, were harmful because the hard plastic strips often scratched the coins as they were slid into and out of the album.

In the present day there are a wide variety of options for storing your coin collection. Here are some beginner-friendly options:

- **2"×2" Cardboard Flips with Mylar Liners:** These inexpensive holders are a staple for new collectors. They're made of cardboard with a window of thin Mylar (a safe, PVC-free plastic) to view the coin. Insert your coin, fold the flap, and secure it with a staple or tape. Be cautious with staples, as they can scratch coins if not flattened down and handled carefully. For extra protection, place a small piece of paper or an envelope between flips to prevent staple scratches.
- **Mylar Flips:** Safe for long-term use but stiff, these PVC-free flips are clear and easy to label. They're ideal for coins that will be handled occasionally and provide good visibility without the risk of chemical breakdown.

- **Plastic Capsules:** For more valuable coins, hard plastic capsules offer excellent protection. These rigid, round, or square holders completely encase the coin, preventing scratches and exposure to air. Available for standard US coin sizes (cents, nickels, dimes, quarters, halves, silver dollars) and some foreign crowns. The nickel size fits half eagles, and the dime size works for quarter eagles and copper-nickel 3-cent pieces. For odd-sized or obsolete coins, place them in polyethylene sleeves first.
  - **Air-Tite and Kointains:** These rigid capsules consist of two shells that snap together around the coin's edge, creating a near-airtight seal. The bowed design prevents surface contact, protecting against scratches and pollutants. Some varieties of Air-Tite capsules include a neoprene ring, which grips the coins securely without touching their surfaces. Since you can't write directly on these capsules, insert them into a labeled 2"×2" flip or paper envelope.
  - **Lucite Holders (e.g., Capital Plastics):** These hard, clear acrylic holders are virtually airtight and extremely durable—perfect for display or long-term storage. Coins are held securely without surface contact, but slight variations in coin diameter mean some may fit tightly while others rattle. Use for coins that match the holder's exact size to avoid edge damage.
- **Coin Albums:** Perfect for displaying multiple coins, coin albums can have clear, protective slides for viewing. Ensure the album is made of archival-quality, PVC-free materials to prevent chemical damage. Albums are great for organizing sets, like state quarters or Lincoln cents, but check periodically for signs of wear or moisture buildup.
- **Slabs for High-Value Coins:** If you own rare or valuable coins, consider professional grading and encapsulation by services like PCGS or NGC. These "slabs" are tamper-proof, airtight holders that protect coins and verify their authenticity and condition.

**What to Avoid:** Never use PVC-based plastic holders, such as soft vinyl flips, for long-term storage. Over time, PVC breaks down, releasing chlorine that forms a green slime on coins, especially copper or silver ones. This can permanently damage the coin's surface. If you notice this green film, remove the coin carefully and clean it with acetone (following the product's instructions, or see Chapter 3) to prevent further harm. Also, steer clear of regular plastic bags, rubber bands, or non-archival paper, as they may contain chemicals that harm coins. Avoid acetate flips, which are brittle and prone to cracking at folds or edges.

For more information about these options, see Chapter 4, "Safe and Simple Coin Storage."

(Left) Some products on the market claim to help control tarnish when placed in a storage receptacle along with the coins. Bags of silica gel can reduce humidity, but they must be replaced regularly.

(Below) Never just hide your coins in the attic or in your dresser under your shirts.

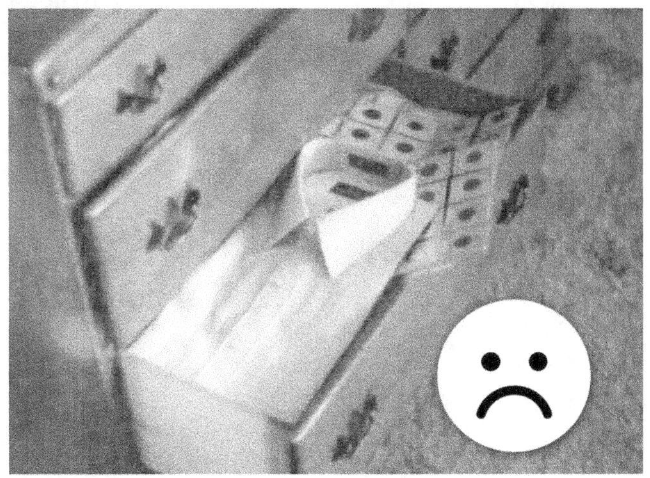

## Safe and Sound

How and where you store your coins is just as important as collecting them in the first place. We should always keep in mind that we are only caretakers of these numismatic treasures, and we want to protect them for the collectors of the future. In other words, how we handle and care for these coins while they are in our possession will impact the collectability of those coins in the future. If they are improperly handled or stored on our watch, they will be permanently affected—never the same again. It's somewhat akin to trying to unring a bell. All collectors should be cognizant of this responsibility.

Coins should be stored as far away from heat and humidity as possible. Both of these factors, particularly when combined, have a very negative effect on numismatic collectibles. A safe-deposit box in your bank is probably one of the best places to keep your coins, provided it is dry and not subject to severe variations in temperature. Some products on the market claim to help control tarnish when placed in the storage receptacle along with the coins. Bags of silica gel retard humidity but must be replaced regularly.

Storing your collection at home can be risky. If your collection is especially valuable, you should install a reliable home-security system. A good, fireproof combination safe is a wise purchase. It's a good idea to conceal it in a closet or another piece of furniture so as not to draw attention to it.

If you don't have the added security of a safe, be sure to store your coins in a well-hidden place, out of sight of cleaners, repairmen, exterminators, or anyone else who has access to your home. Lock your coins in a file or desk drawer. Don't merely hide them in the attic or in your dresser drawer under your shirts.

Again, be sure to check your coins periodically to make certain they are not exposed to chemical hazards. Don't assume that everything is okay just because your coins were fine the last time you inspected them.

Take care of your coins. Even if you're a seasoned numismatist, it doesn't hurt to be reminded of the dos and don'ts of coin collecting. Sometimes we overlook the obvious! Remember, everyone is a darned fool at least five minutes of every day. Even the wise man cannot avoid the occasional pitfall.

# Coin Cleaning Basics

Coin cleaning divides the collecting world like few other topics. One camp sees it as a way to reveal a coin's true beauty; the other treats any intervention as vandalism that can slash a coin's value overnight. As a new collector, you'll handle cleaned coins sooner or later—and you may want to try it yourself on a cheap find. This guide gives you safe, beginner-friendly options **to try on low-value pieces,** while hammering home the big rule: if a coin might be worth real money, leave it alone or hand it to a pro. Practice on pocket change first, and you'll learn what "too far" looks like without regret.

## Why Cleaning Is Risky (and Often Unnecessary)

Time builds a coin's patina—a thin layer of natural toning that serious collectors often love. Strip it away, and you're left with a coin that looks wrong under a loupe: overly bright, artificially smooth, or missing microscopic flow lines from the Mint die. Some third-party grading services do not give a numerical grade for a cleaned coin but actually use a "Details" designation on the slab, and auction prices will follow. For anything beyond everyday, circulated modern coins, the safest move is no move.

## Gentle Methods for Low-Value Coins

Grab a handful of common cents, nickels, or quarters from your change jar. Work over a towel, wear cotton gloves, and use one coin per container to avoid cross-metal contamination.

Be careful when attempting to clean your coins. Hairline scratches can result from improper drying, especially on Proof coins.

*Mild Soap and Water*

The kindergarten of cleaning—safe and effective for light dirt

- In a small bowl, add warm (not hot) water and 2–3 drops of mild, unscented dish soap.
- Swish gently with fingertips or a soft toothbrush for 30–60 seconds.
- Rinse in distilled water (tap water leaves minerals).
- Pat dry with a lint-free, soft cloth or air-dry on a towel—*no rubbing*.

*Vinegar and Salt Soak*

Lifts light tarnish on copper or silver-clad coins

- 1 cup white vinegar + 1 tbsp table salt in a glass/plastic bowl.
- Lay coins flat in a single layer in the bowl, fully covered by the mixture.
- Soak 15–20 minutes max; check often.
- Lightly wipe if needed, then distilled-water rinse and pat dry.

*Acetone Bath*

Removes sticky PVC residue (that green slime from old flips).

- 100 % pure acetone in a small glass jar.
- Soak 5–10 minutes.
- Cool distilled-water rinse; air-dry completely.

*Dipping (Commercial Acid Solutions)*

A quick chemical bath sold at coin shops (e.g., "coin dip" or jewelers' silver cleaner). Use only on modern silver or clad coins, *never* on rare or Proof pieces. Work under ventilation.

- Pour a small amount into a glass dish.
- Hold the coin with plastic tweezers, dip 1–3 seconds, remove immediately.
- Neutralize in a baking-soda water bath (1 tsp soda per cup water) for 10 seconds.
- Rinse in distilled water, then again in acetone or 91% isopropyl alcohol to displace water.
- Air-dry on a soft cloth.

**Warning:** Each dip dissolves a microscopic layer of metal. Repeat too often and luster turns dull and unnatural. Strong drug-store dips are too aggressive; dilute them 2:1 with distilled water or—better yet—skip them entirely.

*Ultrasonic Cleaners*

High-frequency sound waves blast off loose dirt. Reserve for heavily encrusted, low-value bronze or sea-salvage junk, never for Proof or high-grade coins.

- Fill tank with distilled water and add a drop of mild dish soap.
- Place coin in a soft mesh bag or on a silicone mat—never let it rattle against the basket.
- Run 30–60 seconds only, then check progress.
- Immediately rinse in distilled water, then dip in alcohol and air-dry.

**Warning:** Overlong cycles pit or etch surfaces. Combine with a brief dip *only* if you're experienced.

*Olive Oil Soak*

Slow but safe for dirty ancient bronze or copper duplicates.

- Small glass jar, pure olive oil just covering one coin.
- Seal and leave 1–3 days for light grime, up to 1 week for stubborn verdigris.
- Every 24 hours, remove, inspect, and gently prod hard green spots with a soft toothpick.
- When clean, wipe excess oil with a soft cotton cloth, then dip in an acetone or alcohol bath to remove residue.
- Air-dry.

**Warning:** This does not work well on brass or copper-nickel—it may even darken them. Never wipe a Mint State surface; oil removal alone can impart hairlines.

## Universal Warnings

- No wiping or rubbing with abrasives: Toothpaste, baking soda, erasers, or metal polish scratch and scream, "Cleaned!"
- Preserve patina: Stop the moment a coin starts to look unnaturally shiny.
- Rinse thoroughly: Trapped chemicals cause spots later.
- One metal per batch: Silver particles in dip can plate copper coins and vice versa.

## When to Go Pro

Rare, old, or Uncirculated coins require controlled environments. There are three trusted names in professional coin conservation:

- ANACS—Grades and conserves problem coins, including those already cleaned or corroded. Full details and pricing on their website.

- NGC / Numismatic Conservation Services (NCS)—Removes PVC residue, tarnish, carbon spots, and encrustation without harming original surfaces. Conserved coins move seamlessly to NGC grading. Official conservator for the ANA and PNG.
- PCGS—Provides conservation and restoration services aimed at removing detrimental surface contaminants like PVC residue, dirt, and tape residue to improve a coin's eye appeal without using abrasive, damage-causing techniques.

Always submit coins through official channels. The fee is usually a fraction of the value you protect.

## Bottom Line: When in Doubt, Don't

Part of the pleasure of collecting coins is that their history speaks through their honest wear and toning. If you really want "clean" coins, master these techniques on inconsequential, low-value moderns, and let the pros handle anything worth putting in a grading slab. Your collection—and your wallet—will thank you. Happy hunting!

# Safe and Simple Coin Storage

Preserving the condition and value of your coins is one of the most important steps you can take to enjoy your hobby for years to come. Proper storage protects your coins from damage, corrosion, and loss, ensuring they remain as beautiful and valuable as the day you acquired them. Here we're offering practical, beginner-friendly advice on how to store your coins safely using the right materials, environment, and handling techniques.

## Create the Ideal Storage Environment

Coins thrive in a cool, dry, and stable environment. Moisture, heat, and direct sunlight are your collection's worst enemies, as these can cause tarnishing, corrosion, or fading. Aim for a storage area with low humidity and a consistent temperature, ideally 60–70°F (15–21°C). If you live in a humid climate, consider adding silica gel packs to your storage containers to absorb excess moisture. Avoid basements, attics, or areas near windows where temperature and humidity can fluctuate or sunlight can reach your coins. As mentioned before, for security, a bank safe-deposit box is ideal. If you choose to keep your coins in your home, a climate-controlled room or a closet in the main part of the house is often a good choice.

## Choose the Right Storage Materials

Using the proper holders is critical to keeping your coins safe. A good, short-term way to house coins is in mylar "flips." Be sure the flips contain no plasticizers or softening agents. The most common softening agent is polyvinyl chloride (PVC), which when exposed to heat and/or humidity will quickly turn your coins into green, sticky monstrosities. PVC will eat into the coin's surface and cause irreparable harm, often making once-valuable coins virtually worthless.

Mylar flips without PVC, though chemically safe, are generally stiff and very brittle, and care should be taken when inserting or removing coins. You should bow open the flip's opening to create a larger gap before inserting a coin. Scratches can

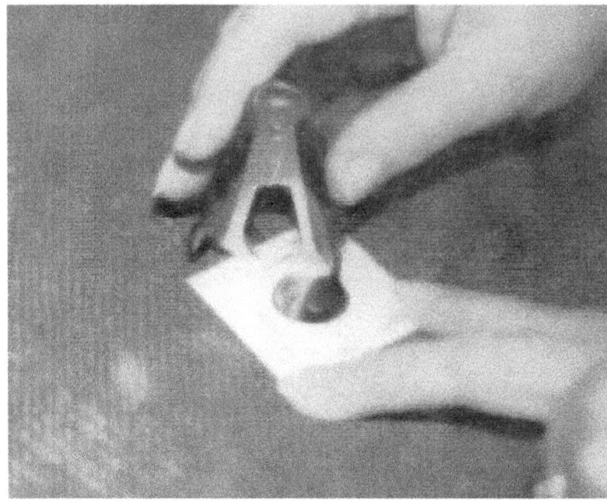

Be sure to take out the staples before attempting to remove coins from cardboard holders. Many coins have been permanently ruined by scratches from staples.

be prevented by first placing the coin in a polyethylene bag and then inserting it in a mylar flip.

Mylar is also used in 2"×2" cardboard holders, which are usually closed with staples. Always flatten the pointed staple ends so they cannot scratch coins in adjacent holders. You can do this by hand using needle-nose pliers to bend the legs flat or—for perfect, effortless results—use a flat clinch stapler. Unlike ordinary staplers that curl the legs inward, flat clinch staplers feature a straight-moving mechanism that presses the staple legs completely flush against the paper. Be sure to take out the staples (usually two will suffice) before attempting to remove coins from these holders. Many coins have been permanently damaged by scratches from staples.

Hard plastic holders are excellent for long-term storage of high-grade collections or even individual coins. These holders should be inspected regularly, though, to ensure that the coins have not deteriorated in any way. A popular holder on the market is the Air-Tite holder, a clear two-piece mylar capsule that fits tightly around the coin and allows you to handle it without actually touching the coin's surfaces. Some versions include a black or white neoprene ring to help hold the coin in place. A similar but now hard-to-find holder, the Kointain capsule, also lacks the black ring. Always be sure you use the holder that exactly matches the coin's diameter to avoid rattling and edge damage.

When a high degree of protection is not required, coins can be stored safely in 2"×2" paper envelopes. Plastic tubes are also excellent for storing rolls of coins. One of the more popular tubes is translucent and squared on the outside to make stacking easier. Coin albums are also an excellent option for displaying multiple coins and organizing whole sets.

When a high degree of protection is not required, coins can be stored safely in 2"×2" paper envelopes.

The encapsulated products offered by virtually all of the third-party grading services protect coins from improper handling but do have some negative features. First, because they are sonically sealed, holders can sometimes trap unnoticed contamination in with the coin. If you spot such contamination, there's nothing you can do to halt a chemical reaction but break open the holder, which voids the grading opinion—but better to have to get the coin graded again than have it ruined by the contamination. Second, the holders generally conceal the edge—that important third side—of the encapsulated coin (though some holders only partially conceal the edge instead, with a portion remaining visible for easier inspection). Third, many collectors prefer examining the "raw" coin so they can get an unobstructed view of the surfaces, allowing light to reflect directly on the coin itself.

Encapsulated coin with CAC sticker. A protective plastic slab from a third-party grading service (PCGS in this instance) displays the coin's certified grade and certification number. The CAC sticker provides independent quality confirmation: green (the so-called "green bean") indicates solid/high-end for the grade; gold suggests potential for a higher grade.

**Note:** Always opt for materials labeled as archival-quality, acid-free, and PVC-free, as these won't react chemically with your coins.

## Check On Your Collection Regularly

Even with the best storage, it's wise to inspect your coins every six months for signs of damage, such as tarnishing, corrosion, or holder deterioration. If you use 2"×2" flips or albums, ensure the Mylar windows haven't cracked or become brittle. For coins in plastic capsules or slabs, check for moisture buildup, especially if stored in a humid environment. Regular checks help you catch issues early and keep your collection in top shape.

# Converging on a Convention

When covering a large bourse floor—such as those at major shows hosted by the ANA, Central States, FUN, Long Beach, or Whitman Expos—in search of varieties (in my case) or specific coins needed for your collection, the experience can feel frustrating or overwhelming. A little preparation, however, can make it a whole lot easier.

When I know I'll be attending a large convention, the first thing I do is make a list of my top priority items—those specific coins or varieties that I most hope to find or ones on a want (or "need") list.

I then try to track down a list of the dealers who will have tables and, if available, a floor plan for where those tables will be located. These can be available on a convention's or show's website or when you register, but sometimes you'll have to wait until you actually get to the convention to obtain one or both of these. If this is the case, plan to arrive at least an hour before the doors open so you can locate this important information and make a game plan.

Once you have the listings and floor plan, find a quiet place where you won't be disturbed so you can go over the names of those dealers you feel might have what you're looking for or whom you want to visit for one reason or another. Highlight those names on the list and their table on the layout with a colored marker for quick identification—I recommend a light-colored marker (yellow, pink, etc.), since some of the numbers on the bourse table maps are so small that they make an eagle squint, and you don't want to obliterate them any further.

When you emerge from your self-designated CIC (Convention Information Center) you'll have in hand your battle strategy—the coins you're most interested in and where to look for them.

Next, unless there is a certain dealer you simply *have to see* as soon as possible, I recommend that you begin your quest systematically by starting at one end of the floor or the other and visiting those tables you've highlighted in order. I usually begin with the lowest-numbered table and work up. Put a big "X" on the floor plan over that dealer's table once you've visited him and seen everything you want to see, so that you'll know he's been covered.

I should mention that I always take with me a small spiral-bound notebook (3"×5"), which lists all the major varieties I'd be interested in by denomination. I do already know most of them without having to refer to this "crib book," but the list is quite long, and I like to have a reminder on occasion. Being small, it's unobtrusive and doesn't cover any stock a dealer might have displayed if you should lay it on the table while you're looking. Just don't forget to take it with you when you leave!

When visiting a dealer's table, there are some points of "Collector Etiquette" I would strongly recommend you follow:

- If the dealer is particularly busy, especially if he's "doing a deal," pass him by and come back later. If you know him, give a wave and let him know you'll be back when he's not occupied. There's no harm in looking at the material he has displayed, though, and making mental notes on what you'd like to see when you return.
- If he's just talking with someone, give his displayed material a quick check and again make a mental note of any items in a particular case you'd like to see. By doing this, it'll be a lot easier for him to get the next coins for you while you are inspecting one instead of waiting between each look-see for you to decide what you want to examine next. If you're fortunate enough to know the dealer well (or if you have a trusting face), he *may* allow you to go through the coins in his case on your own. Let him make this decision, however, and NEVER, EVER OPEN A DEALER'S CASE TO EXAMINE A COIN WITHOUT FIRST ASKING HIM IF YOU CAN DO SO, NO MATTER HOW WELL YOU KNOW EACH OTHER.
- Quite often when looking over coins in a case or in a stock box, if I find a variety that is not marked as such and I have no particular interest in that piece, I'll quietly mention it to the dealer, pointing out what it is and that he could probably get a few dollars more for it if he cared to. I don't do this all the time (have to leave some cherries for the next picker), but it can help to break the ice, especially if a dealer seems stand-offish or suspicious about what you're looking for.
- If the dealer is not busy and you're the only one at the table, there's nothing wrong in striking up a conversation with him—and it doesn't necessarily have to be about coins. If, for instance, he's wearing a Kansas City Royals shirt, chances are fairly good that he's a fan and that's a possible topic for palaver. You'll be able to tell early on if he's in a talking mood or not, so use a little common sense and don't force the issue. And don't stay longer than you should—his attitude will clue you in on this. If he becomes fidgety or quiet for no apparent reason, it's probably time to purchase what you've set aside and quietly leave.

- And for heaven's sake, don't forget to thank him for allowing you to look and for spending time with you—whether you buy anything or not. "I really appreciate you letting me look through your stock. I'm sorry I didn't find anything I could use," is a goodbye I often use.
- It's always a good idea to have in mind certain coins or series that you'd like to concentrate on (Washington quarters or Shield nickels, for instance) beforehand. That way, if the dealer has stock boxes available you can ask if he has any of those coins that you could look over. Again, if he's busy, try to stop back for this part of your search. **Tip:** A clever way to let dealers know exactly what you're hunting—especially for a specific date/mint or tough variety—is to make a simple, handwritten sign on a piece of paper with the name of the coin you're seeking (for example, "Mint State 1927-S Standing Liberty quarter"), as my friend Chet Hogan once suggested. Hold the sign in your hand, clearly visible, as you walk past tables. Many dealers will spot it, and if they have the coin (or something close), they'll often wave you over or call out to you. This saves you from having to explain your want at every single table and lets busy dealers help you without interrupting their current customer.
- If, after selecting the coins I want to purchase, the dealer asks me what I found, I'll usually tell him, and even show him where to look on the coin for that and other varieties. By doing this, many dealers will start looking on their own, and in some cases they may save whatever they find for you to check over at the next show. Many times this little "dealer seminar" has paid for itself down the road, as a dealer is going to see a lot more coins than you over the next few weeks or months, and he's now acting, in essence, as your eyes. If he's good enough to do this for you, it's certainly not unreasonable to pay some sort of a premium (if he asks it) for what he's set aside for you.
- After you've covered all the tables you've highlighted on your layout, now you can go back around and look closer at those tables you passed by the first time. Personally, I usually skip over tables where only (or mostly) slabs are displayed, but after cherrypicking a beautiful, slabbed MS-63 1873 Strong Doubled Die Obverse Shield nickel recently at a dealer's shop, it made me wonder how many of these "coffin coins" have unlabeled varieties on them. ANACS, CACG, ICG, NGC, and PCGS will usually identify and label many coin varieties directly on their slabs (though the scope and frequency vary by service, series, and specific variety). This makes holder notations from these graders a valuable resource for locating desirable varieties during bourse floor searches.

There's been some discussion in the past about whether or not to make a "token" purchase from a dealer if he's allowed you to look over his stock and you've found nothing you can use. Many times I have. . . . Many times I have not. There's no hard and fast recommendation on this. You'll have to play it pretty much by ear.

If you don't know the dealer too well and he's been very cooperative, I think a purchase of some kind would be appropriate, particularly if you've taken a lot of his time. If, on the other hand, you know each other and he knows what you're looking for (having probably bought coins from him in the past and knowing you will visit his table again in the future), a friendly thank you and, "Hope I'll be able to buy something the next time!" usually suffices.

As the bottom line on covering a major convention, I guess the best advice I could give new and erstwhile collectors is to treat a dealer the same way *you* would expect to be treated if you were on the other side of the table. A wise man once said: "Life is not so short, but what there is *always* time enough for courtesy."

I hope the above has helped you in preparing for your next foray into the wonderful and exciting world of collecting at a major convention. The Collector Etiquette points above really apply to any size convention or show, so remember to keep the dealer in mind when you visit his table—it will more than likely pay off for you in the future.

# 6

# Buying Coins Through the Mail

I would suspect that well more than half the collectors in this country, for one reason or another, purchase the majority of the coins for their collection through the mail—or, these days, more often than not, through a quick link online (that still ends up arriving in your mailbox). Sources such as the numismatic weekly newspapers (*Coin World* and *Numismatic News*) remain two good references, as do *The Numismatist* and *Coinage,* and of course specialty club publications (see Chapter 15 for a list of some of those)—not to mention robust online hubs like CoinWeek, the Newman Numismatic Portal, and eBay's dedicated coin sections. Whatnot and eBay Live offer livestream auctions for real-time buying and selling with interactive bidding and community engagement.This method offers a broad spectrum of choices, and for folks who are not within driving distance of a decent coin shop or who do not have the opportunity to attend various coin conventions (virtually or in-person), it really presents a great alternative to add to their numismatic holdings, whether snapping up a slabbed Morgan dollar from a site like GreatCollections or purchasing a fresh US Mint release direct from their online store.

Buying through the mail, while a relatively uncomplicated process, does require some pre-planning and common sense—especially now, with the added layers of digital security and online package tracking that make the whole thing smoother (but no less in need of a sharp eye).

Comparison shopping is important, but the lowest prices don't necessarily mean the best value. Here are a few tips to consider when looking for a coin to fill that hole in your album:

- Big ads don't always equate to lower prices. Ads cost money, and the dealer has to recoup this expense somehow—whether it's a splashy full-page spread in *Coin World* or a promoted listing on eBay. This is not to say that large advertisers have no lower-priced coins; many do! But generally

speaking, advertisements that only offer a few coins will usually be either higher priced or in a lower grade than advertised. (See Chapter 16, "10 Rules of Thumb for Coin Collecting.")

- If you write to a dealer, a researcher, or a specialist seeking information on a coin or product, please remember to include a SASE (self-addressed, stamped envelope) for their reply. Most dealers and researchers are more than happy to share their knowledge with you, but when it costs them 78¢ (the 2026 Forever stamp rate for a First-Class letter), it's not very considerate on your part. A stamp is just about the least expensive price for information you can possibly get, and hey, it might even score you a personal reply from a fellow enthusiast. Though honestly, today, you're more likely emailing or messaging via their website anyway.
- If you call the dealer, is he or his representative helpful and courteous? (This is a two-way street, incidentally.) After your order is taken, are you thanked for ordering? And if you're chatting via email or their site's live support, does the response come quick and clear, and do orders come with tracking details?
- Was your order filled correctly and promptly? Does the dealer state his return policy in his ad—ideally, something like a 30-day, no-questions-asked window to return, complete with free return shipping? With options like USPS Registered Mail or FedEx now standard for high-value shipments, expect to see shipping details upfront too.
- Is the advertiser a member of ANA (American Numismatic Association) or PNG (Professional Numismatists Guild), and does he display those credentials in his advertisements? This is always a plus, because you then have an organization to which you can register a complaint if you are dissatisfied with a deal and it cannot be resolved through the normal procedure. ANA

offers mediation services, CACG, NGC or PCGS may offer discounts on grading, or there may even be insurance perks that come with membership.

- If a disagreement arises, be sure to give the dealer a reasonable amount of time to research and rectify the situation with you. Remember that many dealers are on the road at least three days a week at shows or viewing and buying collections, so a little understanding and patience in this area is important. That said, with email trails and digital photos, resolving grade disputes has never been easier.
- Try to establish a good working relationship with at least one dealer from whom you've received properly graded coins at a fair price through the mail. Send him your wish list, with a *realistic* price you're willing to pay for each item—many now accept these via email or through their online portals. You'd be surprised how many dealers work from want lists and track down coins for their customers. In many cases, if you've been doing business with them for a while, they may even send coins to you on approval, fully insured and tracked.
- Don't be afraid to ask other collectors what mail-order dealers they've dealt successfully with and would recommend. Check active forums like Reddit's r/coins; the ANA's member community; CoinTalk, a longstanding hub for general numismatic discussion; the PCGS message boards, including the US Coin forum and Set Registry forum on Collectors Universe; and the NGC Coin Collectors chat boards for real talk from experienced collectors. These platforms offer expert advice on US, world, and ancient coins, along with specialized discussions on errors, varieties, bullion, grading disputes, pricing trends, and more. (Also ask if you may use their name as a reference if you contact those dealers.)
- Again, refer to Chapter 16, "10 Rules of Thumb for Coin Collecting," later in this book.
- Most important: Enjoy your hobby!

# Bidding at an Auction

If you're planning to attend—or log into—an auction with the intention of bidding on one or more coins and you're new to the game, there are a few things you should know before raising your hand, clicking that bid button, or signaling your proxy bidder—even if the auctioneer on the livestream is a charmer! You should also be aware that an auction is a place where you're liable to end up getting something for nodding off during a late-night online session; some bidders use a head-nod to bid!

These suggestions apply primarily to larger auctions, but the same steps are applicable to all such sales, be they the local club Zoom meetup, a regional hybrid event, or a major international auction, with big players logging in from around the globe. If you heed these recommendations, it'll allow you to enjoy the numismatic auction experience a great deal more, and you'll be more apt to snag the coins for which you lust at the right price.

First, obtain a copy of the auction catalog if there is one—most are digital PDFs available through online platforms these days—and review it carefully, making note of the items in which you may be interested. I prefer to record the lot numbers on a separate sheet of paper or in a notes app first, and then after researching and scrutinizing the seller's high-res photos or attending a viewing session, highlight the lot number in the catalog if I'm still interested.

Be certain to read the auction rules very carefully and completely beforehand so you know as much as possible about the auction. Is it a hybrid affair, with floor, phone, internet, and proxy bidding (meaning collectors who can't make it in person can submit max bids online ahead of time), or is it strictly livestreamed for remote bidders? What commission (often called "the juice") will be added to your winning bid to help the auction house cover their costs? This buyer's premium generally runs 10–25% these days, depending on the house and format. Are floor or online bids considered final (non-returnable, except for authenticity issues)? What forms of payment are accepted—cash, check, credit card (up to certain limits), wire transfer, ACH, or even PayPal for smaller lots? Can you pay and ship your wins immediately after the hammer falls, or is there a checkout window? When and where will the lots be viewable prior to the auction—in person at a viewing room, or via ultra-HD zoomable images and sometimes 360-degree spins online? Are all lots guaranteed as described, with authenticity backed by the major houses? How can you access the "Prices Realized" list after the sale (usually posted online within days, free for all)?

Once you've done your preliminary homework and have flagged the lots in which you have an interest, you need to determine what you're willing to pay for those pieces. There are several solid sources that will provide you with a "guideline" in this respect. *Greysheet* is still a trusty reference as it lists Bid and Ask parameters for virtually every US coin you may need, in just about every grade—now in a slick digital edition. Other go-tos include the PCGS Price Guide and NGC Coin Explorer for real-time market data and archives of past sales from sites like Heritage Auctions, Stack's Bowers, or GreatCollections. Has the coin in which you're interested gone under the hammer before, and, if so, when, and what did it fetch (adjusted for inflation and market shifts)? Ads in trade papers, online marketplaces like eBay's sold listings, and even AI-powered valuation tools in apps will also give you a guide on the current market value. In short, the more information you can assemble via apps, databases, and forums in regard to the going price on your wanted coin, the better equipped you are to consider if you can afford the coin and what you want to pay.

Armed with this important information, and after viewing the coins—whether through crystal-clear online images or hands-on inspection—to ensure that in your opinion they are genuine and properly graded, you must now set a maximum price you're willing to pay and note that price next to the appropriate lot number in your catalog or bidding app. Remember, you must figure in the buyer's premium (again, 10–25% of the winning bid!) plus shipping charges to arrive at your maximum. *Never* buy a coin without first examining it (or its digital twin)! Coins encapsulated by independent third-party grading services like ANACS, CACG, ICG, NGC, or PCGS stand a better chance (in most cases) of being the grade listed, but even then, remember you're buying the coin, not the slab—or the pixelated photo.

Once you have established the maximum total you can pay, stick to it. Emotion plays a major part in any auction, and it's very easy to become overly emotional, especially during a frenzied live chat or if you particularly want the coin for your collection. The worst thing you can do is overextend your resources just because you "need" that coin! If you're not able to purchase it now, most likely the opportunity will present itself again down the road—numismatics moves fast online.

There is a great deal of psychology in bidding from the floor, phone, or screen. Some folks (the "Statue of Liberty" bidder) jump in early and stay aggressive until they win or hit their limit. Others "lie in the digital bullrushes" with a proxy max bid and let the platform handle the increments automatically. Still others lurk in the chat shadows or use subtle paddle raises in the room, attempting anonymity from the other bidders (though bidder IDs online can give them away). What method you use is up to you, but . . . .

If possible, spectate one or two auctions before starting to bid—whether virtually tuning in via simulcast or showing up in person—just to see what goes on, how things flow in real time, and how you feel is the best way for you to bid on your lots. Be observant!

Once you are successful in your bidding, it goes without saying—but I'll say it anyway—you must be able to pay for your purchases in full and promptly, often within 24 to 72 hours via a secure portal. Don't try to cut a deal with the auction house for "time payments," etc. They must pay their consignors promptly, and it's not fair to all parties not to settle up on time, especially if international shipping is in the mix.

Auctions can be fun and very rewarding. Here's a tip: after scrutinizing the individual lots in which you're interested (online or off), if you have time, check the "bulk lots" that usually wrap up the catalog. Many times there are some jewels lurking amongst these large lots, and they can be won at a very attractive price—especially if you're savvy with a quick lot scan using your phone's magnifier app. Knowledge is power, but applying that knowledge—spotting the hidden gems, acting fast, and turning insight into a winning bid—is the real superpower!

# Tips on Mailing Coins

Many people do not ship high-value items often, so this information might be of particular value to new collectors. Sooner or later, each of us is going to be sending coins through the mail, whether to other collectors or specialists for attribution or returns to dealers that are not acceptable. They may be worth only a few dollars or a few thousand dollars, but whatever their value, you'll want to protect them in the best way possible to make certain they arrive at their destination safely and in good condition.

## Packaging

Many valuable coins are lost in the mail as a result of improper packaging.

If you're sending just a few coins, they may be housed in a "SAFE-T-MAILER," a sticky, corrugated cardboard enclosure. Alternatively, they may be placed carefully between two pieces of heavy cardboard such as the back of a pad of paper, and stapled shut (remembering to flatten down the staples afterward). For added security, slip those coins into protective flips or slabs first to prevent scratches or rattles. Not only do coins get lost through improper packing, but even more are damaged because someone didn't take a little extra time to properly protect them. The SAFE-T-MAILER or cardboard holder containing the coins may now be placed in a regular envelope (though the heavier the better), providing the coins are not too heavy or bulky. If this is the case, a small box—again with the coins well protected—should be used. Make sure they do not rattle around in the box. I've seen too many beauties come back dinged from sliding around. SAFE-T-MAILERS are readily available at your local coin supply house, or online from places like Wizard Coin Supply if your neighborhood shop is short on stock.

When using a box, make sure it is sturdy enough to withstand the trip through our postal system—sorting machines haven't gotten any gentler over the years. It's a good idea to protect the coins using bubble wrap, foam inserts, or even those eco-friendly packing "noodles" instead of Styrofoam peanuts to keep things quiet and secure. Tape the box securely with heavy-duty filament tape prior to wrapping with additional outer wrap. I've found a large, recycled paper shopping bag or plain brown paper does a very adequate job for wrapping, and you should use reinforced brown KRAFT tape (either the kind you moisten or the self-sealing variety) on the outside. You can probably find this type of tape at your local office supply store, Amazon, or big-box shops like Walmart. Don't skimp on the tape—too much is better than too little. Brown Kraft tape is preferred over shiny packing tape so that the post office stamp can be affixed to it without smearing, and it meets USPS guidelines for Registered Mail. Clear plastic tape or duct tape is not ideal for Registered, as it can complicate inspections. When packaging, try to think about the person opening the package. You wouldn't want them to damage the coins when opening the package—maybe add a note on the box saying, "Open with care."

Address the package carefully and make sure your return address is properly displayed—use a printed label if handwriting's not your strong suit. Be sure to enclose an invoice and keep a copy for your records, perhaps with photos of the coins for good measure, in case of disputes.

The above instructions apply to both Insured and Registered/Insured letters and packages. It's also a good idea to overlap your stamps and/or Registered or Insured number sticker on your address label. By doing so, no one can place another address over yours and have it sent to the address of their choice. When sending coins for identification or attribution, be sure to obtain permission first (don't forget to include a self-addressed, stamped envelope), and include enough money for return postage and insurance when sending the coin(s). And a tip from the digital age: Track everything online via your carrier's website; it's free and gives you peace of mind without keeping track of the old paper stubs.

## Types of Coverage (USPS)

*Insured First Class, Priority Mail, Priority Mail Express:*

(Note: The following prices are accurate as of January 25, 2026. They will necessarily have to be updated as postal rates change.)

While the maximum coverage on Insured Mail is now $5,000, it is suggested that any coins/valuables worth more than $500 be sent via Registered/Insured Mail. A quick check of the rates in the two tables that follow will confirm that this is the prudent action to take, as Registered Mail is more secure than Insured Mail. Services like Priority Mail and Priority Mail Express now include up to $100 of basic insurance for free, but for coins, always opt to add on coverage for the full declared value—numismatics can be tricky with claims, so *declare accurately*.

The current rates for additional Insured First Class (beyond any included coverage) are approximately

| **Liability Range** | **Fee** |
|---|---|
| $0.01 to $50.00 | $2.75 |
| $50.01 to $100.00 | $3.50 |
| $100.01 to $200.00 | $4.60 |
| $200.01 to $300.00 | $6.05 |
| $300.01 to $400.00 | $5.95 to $5.80 (varies by source) |
| $400.01 to $500.00 | $7.45 |
| $500.01 to $5,000.00* | Rates increase by approximately $1.50 per $100 of coverage above $500 |

*Liability for insured mail is limited to $5,000.00.

Insured First Class parcels are signed for by the recipient (or his or her agent) upon delivery, and the post office retains the yellow (acknowledgment) slip. When mailing the package, the sender retains a portion of the form affixed to the package, which includes the insurance number of the package, the amount for which it was insured, the date it was sent, and the destination city. You should fill in the top portion yourself, indicating the name of the person and the full address to which it is being sent. **Note:** Newer insurance forms also include a section for the name of the recipient and the full address, and you can now buy and print labels online via Click-N-Ship for electronic tracking.

Claims may be filed on lost packages after a prescribed period following mailing (usually 60 days), and the total insured amount will be recovered by the sender if the parcel is not located. Be advised, this takes time to process—often up to three months—and for coins, you'll need solid proof of value, such as appraisals or market quotes.

*Registered Mail*

This is by far the safest way to send merchandise through the postal system, although it is quite a bit more expensive. You must send your coins and other valuables this way if you want coverage for over $5,000. USPS will cover up to a maximum of $25,000 per package now, which covers most collector shipments without breaking the bank.

The current rates for Registered/Insured mail are approximately

| **Liability Range** | **Fee*** |
|---|---|
| $0.01 to $100.00 | $10.80 |
| $100.01 to $500.00 | $12.10 |
| $500.01 to $1,000.00 | $13.30 |
| $1,000.01 to $2,000.00 | $14.50 |
| $2,000.01 to $3,000.00 | $15.70 |
| $3,000.01 to $4,000.00 | $16.90 |
| $4,000.01 to $5,000.00 | $18.10 |
| $5,000.01 to $50,000.00 | $18.10 + handling charge of $1.20 per each $1,000 or fraction thereof over $5,000 |

*Fees for articles valued over $25,000 are for handling only. Maximum amount of insurance coverage available is $25,000.

These fees are for Registered insurance only. Postage for the package is additional—add First-Class, Priority, or Ground Advantage based on speed requirements. **Note:** Check with your local post office for higher coverage rates and for updates on increased fees. Online tools like the USPS Rate Calculator can give you an exact quote in seconds.

The major difference from Insured First Class is that Registered Mail is accounted for and signed for at each location along the route to the recipient. Postal employees are therefore a good deal more conscientious when handling Registered Mail, because they are held accountable for it by way of their signature. Any lost article can be traced to the point where the receipt signature ceased—it's a digital breadcrumb trail, with scans at every handoff.

Again, the recipient signs a yellow slip upon receipt, and the post office retains the form. The receipt the sender keeps at the time he or she mails the package is much more complete than that for Insured First Class mail, as it lists full addresses of both the sender and the recipient; the registry number of the parcel; the total cost breakdown, including the amount it is registered for; and as on the Insured, the round post office date stamp.

**Never send coins or anything of value by Certified Mail!** This method offers no monetary protection whatsoever, and if lost you cannot recover any part of the value. It is strictly a method to ensure a certain letter or parcel is delivered—nothing more. If a package is lost, you have no recourse. Stick to Certified for documents, not treasures.

*Return Receipt*

For a small additional fee (currently $4.40 for the physical green card, PS Form 3811, or $2.82 for electronic option, Email PDF), you may put a Return Receipt Request card on the letter or package, which, when returned (or emailed), will confirm to you that the package was received. Who accepted it at the other end and the date it was delivered will be included on the form. Go electronic if you can—it's faster and greener and integrates right into your email.

A little extra time spent on packaging and making sure the item is sent in the proper manner will save you a lot of headaches down the road, believe me! With tracking apps and online labels these days, it's easier than ever to ship smart. Just remember, no method is foolproof, so insure like your collection depends on it.

# Grading Hints

## For the Indian 1¢, Lincoln 1¢, Buffalo 5¢, Jefferson 5¢, Mercury 10¢, Roosevelt 10¢, Standing Liberty 25¢, Washington 25¢, Walking Liberty 50¢, Franklin 50¢, Kennedy 50¢, Morgan $1, and Peace $1

This chapter introduces the grading characteristics of several popular US coin series: Indian and Lincoln cents; Buffalo and Jefferson nickels; Mercury and Roosevelt dimes; Standing Liberty and Washington quarters; Walking Liberty, Franklin, and Kennedy half dollars; and Morgan and Peace dollars.

Before examining these series individually, the collector must understand the Mint State (MS) grading scale, which forms the foundation for grading all Uncirculated coins. Mint State coins show no wear, but they vary widely in surface preservation, luster, strike, and eye appeal. The MS-60 through MS-70 scale provides a structured way to evaluate these differences and develop consistent judgment in grading.

For beginners, these grade descriptions need to serve as reference points, not rigid categories. Coins within the same numeric grade may range from low-end to high-end examples. Experience with a specific series is essential, but knowledgeable graders generally operate within a narrow range of consensus.

Keep the following principles in mind:

- Technique over memorization. Learn how to evaluate coins, not just how to label them.
- Subjectivity has limits. Grading is opinion, but it is informed opinion by experienced professionals within accepted standards. These opinions generally won't vary too much from a certain center point.
- Ownership bias exists. Owning a coin can inflate its perceived grade by as much as a point and a half. We all want to believe our coin is the best.
- Quality exists at every grade. Each grade includes low-, mid-, and high-end examples; always try to seek coins at the upper end of the assigned grade. To do this, we must develop confidence in our own grading skills.

## How to Examine a Coin

- Hold the coin over a soft surface (a notebook, paper, or cloth) in case it slips.
- Begin by viewing the coin with **the naked eye** to assess overall eye appeal. Most of the time, your initial, naked-eye impression will hold true after magnification. If you don't like the coin without a loupe, you probably won't like it any better with one. This step is the best way to judge eye appeal right away.
- Use a 5× or (preferably) a 7× loupe. As mentioned in Chapter 2, a Hastings Triplet is worth the extra cost to avoid peripheral distortion common in cheaper models. Higher magnification than 7×, though, is overkill, limiting the viewing area too much to be useful.
- Use proper lighting. Traditional incandescent lamps (75–100 watts) were long favored for their excellent color rendering and warm light that reveals luster, toning, and surface details accurately. Since those bulbs are largely unavailable, high-CRI (90+ or ideally 95+) LED lamps are the best modern replacement. Choose warm white (2700K–3000K) to mimic incandescent glow, or natural daylight (4000K–5000K) for enhanced contrast. Avoid standard low-CRI LEDs or fluorescents, which can mislead on color and wear.
- Use the "T-n-T" method—tip-n-turn the coin for a better view. Hold the coin by the edge and slowly tip and rotate it under the light. This sweeps reflected light across the surfaces, revealing slide marks, subtle wear on high points, hairlines, and luster quality that may not show when the coin is viewed flat.
- Examine the edge—the coin's "third side"—for rim nicks, scratches, or other defects.
- Always handle others' coins with the same care as your own—by the edges only, with plenty of respect.

The more coins you look at, the more proficient you will become. Concentrate on learning one or two series thoroughly first; the same techniques apply across all series. The following sections will give you a good overview of what particular points to focus on for each series as you learn to grade and analyze these coins. As my good friend Ken Bressett has always said, grading is very simple. All you need is four things: a good loupe, proper lighting, good memory, and 20 years' experience.

**Note:** Since 2007, the Certified Acceptance Corporation (CAC) will review already-certified coins and award green "bean" stickers to those that meet or exceed strict quality standards within their assigned grade. In rarer cases, coins considered to be undergraded by the original service and deemed to exceed the assigned grade receive a gold sticker instead. CAC-stickered coins—epecially those with green or gold beans—often command premiums because they indicate high-end examples for the grade.

## Mint State Grade Descriptions

With your examination technique in place, here are the standard descriptions for Mint State grades, summarizing those commonly used in the industry and reflected in the *Official American Numismatic Association Grading Standards for United States Coins.*

**Note:** The ANA has not established official adjectival equivalents for MS-60 through MS-70. Commercial usage often refers to MS-63 as "Choice Uncirculated" and MS-65 as "Gem Uncirculated." Copper coins graded MS/PF-60 or higher should also have their color designated as Red, Red Brown, or Brown.

**MS-70**: A perfect coin. Exceptional strike and original luster; no marks, hairlines, or defects under magnification. Outstanding eye appeal. Copper coins are fully bright, with full original color and luster.

**MS-69**: Very sharp strike and full luster, with no more than one or two tiny, non-detracting marks or flaws. No hairlines. Exceptional eye appeal. Copper coins are bright, with full original color and luster.

**MS-68**: Sharp strike and full luster. Up to four light, scattered contact marks; no visible hairlines or scuff marks. Exceptional eye appeal. Copper coins have lustrous original color.

**MS-67**: Full luster and sharp strike. A few very small contact marks and possibly one more noticeable but non-detracting mark. One or two small hairlines or partially hidden scuffmarks may show under magnification. Exceptional eye appeal. Copper coins have lustrous original color.

**MS-66**: Above-average strike and full original Mint luster. No more than two or three minor (but noticeable) contact marks. A few light hairlines or one or two scuffmarks may show under magnification on frosted surfaces or in the field. Eye appeal is clearly above average and very pleasing. Copper coins display full original or lightly toned color (as designated).

**MS-65**: Attractive, high-quality luster and strike. A few small, scattered contact marks or two larger ones; one or two small patches of hairlines are visible under magnification. Light scuffmarks may show on high points. Overall quality is above average, with very pleasing eye appeal. Copper coins have full luster with original or darkened color (as designated).

**MS-64**: At least average luster and strike. Several small contact marks (possibly grouped) and one or two moderately heavy marks. One or two small patches of hairlines visible under low magnification. Light scuffmarks or defects may appear in the design or field. Attractive overall quality, with pleasing eye appeal. Copper coins may be slightly dull; color should be designated.

**MS-63**: Mint luster may be slightly impaired. Numerous small contact marks and a few scattered heavy ones are visible. Small hairlines visible without magnification. Several detracting scuffmarks or defects are seen throughout. General quality is only about average, but the coin remains fairly attractive. Copper pieces may be darkened or dull; color should be designated.

**MS-62**: Impaired or dull luster. Clusters of small marks with a few large ones or nicks in prime focal areas. Hairlines are very noticeable. Large, unattractive scuffmarks on major features. Strike, rim, and planchet quality may be noticeably below average. Eye appeal is generally acceptable. Copper coins show diminished color and tone.

**MS-61**: Noticeably impaired luster, with clusters of large and small contact marks. Hairlines very noticeable. Scuffmarks as unattractive patches on large areas or major features. Small rim nicks, striking, or planchet defects may show; quality is noticeably poor. Eye appeal is somewhat unattractive. Copper pieces are generally dull, dark, and possibly spotted.

**MS-60**: Unattractive, dull, or washed-out Mint luster. Many large, detracting contact marks or damage spots, but no trace of wear. Heavy concentration of hairlines or large areas of scuffmark visible. Rim nicks may be present. Eye appeal is very poor. Copper coins may be dark, dull, and spotted.

These Mint State benchmarks apply to all series, but each design has unique challenges due to strike characteristics, metal composition, and wear patterns on the high points. The sections that follow focus primarily on MS-60 through MS-65—the grades of greatest interest and uncertainty for most collectors.

For visual references and to learn more about Circulated grades, consult established guides like the *The Official American Numismatic Association Grading Standards for United States Coins* by Kenneth Bressett and Q. David Bowers or *Making the Grade: A Grading Guide to the Top 50 Most Widely Collected U.S. Coins* by Beth Deisher and Michael Fahey. PCGS Photograde Online (www.pcgs.com/photograde) is an excellent free resource with thousands of high-resolution images of PCGS-graded coins to help you match what you're holding.

With these standards, techniques, and resources in hand, you're well prepared to evaluate the specific grading characteristics of each series ahead.

# Grading Hints for the Indian Cent (1859–1909)

On all copper coins, color is an essential ingredient in grading both Uncirculated and Circulated specimens, but for different reasons.

Color on Uncirculated pieces is described in three adjectival ways by the various grading services. Those coins exhibiting full, natural, original golden/orange color are designated "Red." Those pieces that still have a majority of the original golden/orange attractiveness showing but with some patches of brown are labeled "Red-Brown," and specimens that have just a bit of the original color surrounded by a natural (brown) oxidation or are completely a rich, chocolate color are dubbed "Brown."

"Red" coins in any particular Mint State grade command a significant premium, as this original shine and state of preservation over the years is scarce and much desired. Many dates in the Indian cent series in MS-65 Red are valued many times the price of the same grade in Brown or even Red-Brown. Because of these wide pricing variations, and because there are different degrees of color, especially in the Red-Brown classification, I have long felt that there should be a more accurate way to classify the coins that fall into this area.

Under the present practice, if a coin does not have full, blazing, original color, or if it is not almost completely void of any of the original color, it falls into the Red-Brown category by the grading services. Just like a given Mint State grade, in which there are low-end, mid-range, and high-end specimens for the particular grade, so too are there quality variations in color within the Red-Brown designation.

As a suggestion—and I fully realize we're in a *very* subjective area here—leaving the qualifications for the "Red" attribution alone, and describing as "Brown" only those specimens that show no gold/orange color at all, perhaps we should open up the "Red-Brown" parameters to a three-tiered designation:

- **Red/Red-Brown ("RRB")**: coins displaying most of the original golden/orange color, but interrupted by one or more areas of darker toning on either the obverse or reverse (or both).
- **Red-Brown ("RB")**: the present designation used. Coins that would qualify for this description should have about half the original color, with the balance the darker, oxidized red or brown.
- **Red-Brown/Brown ("RBB")**: most of the coins in this descriptive category would be brown, with only traces of the original color showing through.

If accepted, these new designations might make the dramatic price differences between Red, Red-Brown, and Brown a bit easier to understand and accept. It's just a thought. . . .

I mentioned at the top of the article that color also plays an important (but different) part in Circulated specimens. I have never felt that color (or more precisely, the difference in color) has been stressed enough in determining a Mint State coin from one with wear on it. The Indian cent is a great object lesson coin in this respect. The first area(s) to change color on the Indian cent are

- **Obverse:** The hair above the ear, the cheek, and lowest hair curl just behind the ribbon.
- **Reverse:** The knot of the bow, the acorns, and outside edges of the leaves.

These are the areas of highest relief on this coin and, as such, are obviously the first points where wear (circulation) will manifest itself. What you should look for in these critical areas is a dullness in color which may be darker or lighter. The important thing to recognize is the difference from the surrounding area. The change in color is the result of the loss of the original Mint luster, and this fact is true on all coins—look for the difference in color or luster to identify wear. Closer examination will often show that this is accompanied by a loss of detail in the design in these areas. As the coin receives more wear from circulation, these worn, darker areas will expand, and the color change will be more noticeable.

Quite often you will see a Mint State or high-grade Circulated piece (such as AU-55 or 58) with a flatness on the lowest curl behind the ribbon and/or the tops of the feathers on the Indian's headdress. Often this is the result of inadequate striking pressure, and the easiest way to tell is to (again) check the color. If the weakness or apparent wear is due to a weak strike, those areas will not have the dullness associated with wear, but instead will show the original *planchet* luster. A weak strike should be essentially the same color as the rest of the coin.

Because the Indian cent is a portrait coin, with the obverse the real deal breaker in grading—the "money side," if you will—you should inspect the cheek very carefully for slide marks or hairline scratches. Often these scratches are difficult to find, but so many coins with a broad cheek area have hairlines from improper cleaning, drying, or handling. Any buyer needs to be particularly careful in their inspection. All the grading services are very strict regarding hairlines, regardless of how subtle, and it will be wise for you to develop a mindset of, "They're there; go find 'em!" If you realize this and then *don't* find any after (1) tipping and turning the coin (2) in good lighting (3) under proper magnification (7×), you're probably home free in this regard.

**Note:** I have a tendency to prefer one side over the other when determining grades for any series. On the Indian cent, I feel it is easier to pick up wear on the obverse and then confirm my findings by checking the reverse.

Refer to Chapter 11 on weak strikes to learn about those in this series that usually are not fully struck, and to Chapter 14 for reference books about this coin.

# Grading Hints for the Lincoln Cent (1909–2025)

Like other copper coins, Mint State Lincoln cents are adjectivally qualified by the "Red," "Red-Brown," and "Brown" designations. Please refer to my comments about this in the section on Indian cents. As in the Indian cent series—and any other coin—a difference in color/luster is a vital factor in determining a Circulated piece from a Mint State specimen.

The first points of wear in this series (again, I prefer to look at the obverse first) are

- **Obverse:** The cheek and jawbone, the hair above the ear, and the leading edge of the lapel.
- **Reverse:** The lower wheat stalks (1909–1958) and the top of the Memorial building (1958–2008). For later issues, check the specific high points of the design—e.g., cabin roof/logs (2009 Birth & Childhood), top of book/Lincoln's head (2009 Formative Years), Capitol dome/roofline (2009 Professional Life and Presidency), or the raised shield elements (2010–2025 Union Shield: vertical stripes, ONE CENT scroll, top motto bar, and shield outline).

Lincoln's cheek and jaw are probably the two easiest areas to identify initial wear on the obverse. Don't forget to tip and turn the coin under a good light while using a good magnifier (7×). You'll see the difference in color—a dullness compared to the surrounding areas—that tells you that the coin has seen some circulation. Again, as in any series, the longer it is in circulation, the broader and flatter these areas will become, and other details will start to show the same effect.

When you're inspecting a high-grade coin, sometimes these areas that show first points of wear will be shiny rather than dull. This is more than likely due to abrasions from coming in contact with other coins in a roll or bag (metal-against-metal) instead of friction or oils from fingers, so check other areas such as the field to see if you can pick up any luster loss that will tell you if it's Circulated or not.

Refer to Chapter 11 on weak strikes to learn which dates in this series are not usually fully struck, and Chapter 14 for reference books about this coin.

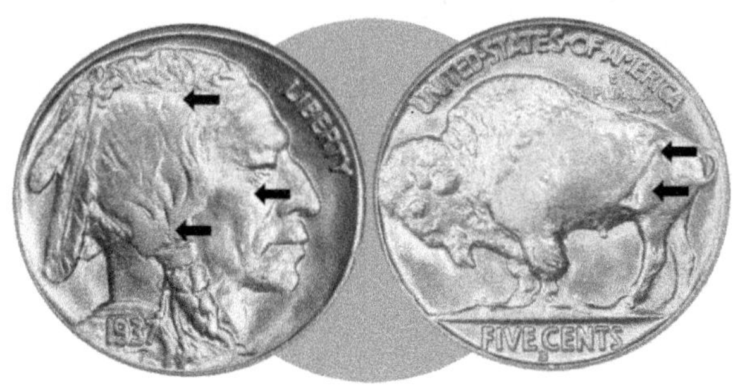


# Grading Hints for the Buffalo Nickel (1913–1938)

For the Buffalo nickel, the preferred side to begin inspecting for wear and grade is the reverse. The key areas to look at in this series is the buffalo's hipbone and the flank underneath it. If the hipbone shows a "Mesa Effect," it is technically not Mint State. This mesa effect is illustrated in drawings of a cross-section of the buffalo's hip.

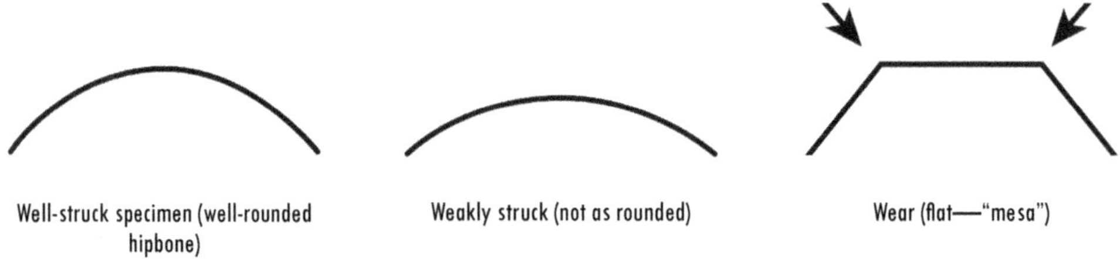


Look closely for the flatness on the hipbone, which—when accompanied by a dullness in color on this spot and the flank underneath—denotes wear. If there is a hip flatness but it is shiny instead, this could be the result of coin-against-coin abrasions in the roll and could still be Mint State. When in doubt, check that flank for the confirmation that it is not. Don't ignore the obverse, but if there is wear on the reverse in this spot, there will be wear on the obverse, particularly on the cheek bone, nose, and braid, though it may be more difficult to see.

Although grading typically begins with the reverse, you must also understand the obverse high points. Check the cheekbone under the eye (the highest point), the hairline and part line, and the braid just above the tie, as these show wear first. Because the braid can appear flat from a weak strike, confirm wear by a change in color or texture—especially if a mesa effect is seen on the buffalo's hip. Wear on the reverse hip and flank will also appear on the cheekbone, nose, and braid, though it may be subtler.

Color/luster is a key factor in all grading, but it is of *utmost* importance on the Buffalo nickel. Because of the nature of the metallic content of this series (75% copper, 25% nickel), a Buffalo nickel need not be fully brilliant to achieve a MS-65 (or better) grade. It must, however, have original luster, be relatively mark-free, and be well struck for the date.

In this series, strike is a very important grading factor. Many of issues struck at branch mints during the late teens and early- to mid-twenties are horribly struck, the result of using the dies well past their effectiveness for proper striking. The same is true for many of the 1935 Denver and San Francisco products, and some latitude is necessary when grading these coins. A fully struck or well-struck piece will show an incused depression just above the tie on the braid on the obverse. Weaker-struck specimens will have this area flat, with no such definition. On the reverse, the areas of weakness are the buffalo's upper front leg and shoulder, and the hair on the head in front of the horn. These are areas of highest relief on the coin (deepest portions of the die) and are therefore the last parts of the design to strike up.

Generally speaking, the better the strike, the more attractive the luster (or original toning), and the fewer the contact marks, the higher the grade once the coin is determined to be Uncirculated. This, of course, may be said of any series, but the biggest problem here seems to be identifying the difference between About Uncirculated/Brilliant Uncirculated.

A "well-struck" coin is generally considered one that exhibits much more detail on both the obverse and reverse than the majority of that issue. For example, a 1926-D without the mushy, ill-defined appearance, but still not having the sharpness of a fully struck coin, may still be classified as "well struck." Similarly, a 1935-D specimen without the broad, flat, grainy surface on the hair above the braid on the obverse and on the bison's upper leg on the reverse could also still be called "well struck." You should study the striking characteristics for each date and mint. Refer to Chapter 11 on weak strikes for more information.

*Suggested definitions for the various Mint State grades:*

**MS-65, Well Struck:** A coin exhibiting attractive, full, natural luster, with no wear and a minimum of contact marks, none of them detracting. It may have (natural) toning, but the original luster must be present. The "groove" in the hair immediately above the tie on the braid should be well defined on those coins that are generally well struck, but it need not be as prominent on coins that are usually found with weak strikes or struck from worn dies.

**MS-64:** A coin with the above characteristics that is normally weakly struck or struck from worn dies; may have no evidence of the groove above the braid tie.

**MS-63:** A coin that suffers some luster loss and/or has some fairly noticeable contact marks in the prime focal areas. The strike might not be up to par compared to the usual specimens encountered for the date/mintmark.

**MS-60:** A coin with no trace of wear on the hip bone, flank, or hair in front of the horn, but with more than the usual contact marks, impaired or poor luster, or is much more weakly struck than the average.

On Proof Buffalo nickels, very often there will be "flyspecks" spotting them, probably the result of saliva or water droplets falling on the coin years ago. These are also seen on some high-grade Circulation strikes, and they are impossible to remove without destroying the original luster of the coin.

# Grading Hints for the Jefferson Nickel (1938–present)

Hopefully, by now you're getting the picture that a difference in color is just as important as (or more than) the loss of design detail in determining wear on a coin. The Jefferson nickel is no exception—same song, different verse.

Because of the availability of Mint State specimens throughout this series, generally there's not a lot of collector or market interest in Circulated specimens. With a few exceptions (the 1939-D and S and a few of the varieties), the cost of a nice Uncirculated coin is well within just about everyone's reach.

I am usually able to pick up the first, slightest signs of wear (in this case usually manifesting itself by a lighter color) by starting on the reverse in this series. These first areas of wear, or the high points of the design on this coin, are

- **Obverse:**
  - Pre-2004: Jaw, collar, and lower edge of the bust.
  - 2004–2005 Westward Journey: Cheekbone, jawline, and hair above the forehead.
  - 2006–present (forward-facing portrait): Cheekbone, tip of the nose, and hair above the forehead.
- **Reverse:**
  - Pre-2004/2006–present: Triangular area above the columns on Monticello.
  - 2004 Peace Medal: Clasped hands and medal/pipe details.
  - 2004 Keelboat: Sail and mast.
  - 2005 American Bison: Bison shoulder (hump), hip, and leg muscles.

Using the tip-n-turn method when examining for wear, look closely at the triangular area at the top center of the building. In the standard metal composition, a lighter color here will denote wear (the color is usually darker on the Wartime composition issues minted from 1942 to 1945), and your determination can be confirmed by turning to the obverse and checking the above points on the portrait.

There are two important points that should be mentioned when collecting this series: First is the importance of "Full Steps" on the reverse. The Monticello building shows six complete steps when fully struck. Six steps are common on a few dates, and extremely rare on others. The market generally accepts five complete steps as a "Full Step" nickel. If it has six, that's a bonus. The easiest way to determine the step count on a coin is to count the unbroken, incused lines in the step area. The top porch step is step #1, so if you can count five complete lines, unbroken by contact marks or a weak strike, you have a six-step nickel. Four complete lines equate to a five-step piece, and so on. In just about every case, the fullness of the steps is a feature of the strike. Generally speaking, the fuller the strike and the fresher the dies, the higher the step count.

Collectors should be aware that all 1938-P, D, and S, and some 1939-P, D, and S issues were struck with what is referred to as "Type of 1938" steps. They are wavy and ill-defined, and this indistinct step separation makes it much more difficult to count exactly how many steps there are. Experience is an important factor in determining the step count on these pieces.

For some dates and mintmarks, a full (five) step count is genuinely rare, and six steps is basically unheard of. These command a significant premium when located in MS-64 or MS-65 with full steps:

- 1953-S
- 1954-S
- 1960-D
- 1961-D
- 1968-D

Other issues are extremely difficult to find with full steps:

- 1944-S
- 1945-S
- 1949-P
- 1953-P
- 1959-D
- 1960-P
- 1961-P
- 1969-D
- 1970-D

Jefferson specialists may add several others to this list.

Another area that should be mentioned is the prevalence of die varieties within the series. The Jefferson nickel offers a full range of important and rare varieties that are very collectible:

- 1939-P Doubled Die Reverse (two different dies)
- 1939 Proof Type of 1940 Steps
- 1940 Proof Type of 1938 Steps

- 1941-S Large S
- 1942-P Doubled Die Obverse (two different dies)
- 1942-D/Horizontal D
- 1943/2-P Overdate
- 1943-P Doubled Die Obverse (Doubled Eye)
- 1945-P Doubled Die Reverse (three different dies)
- 1946-D/Inverted D
- 1946-S Doubled Die Obverse
- 1949-D/S Overmintmark
- 1951 Proof Doubled Die Obverse
- 1953 Proof Doubled Die Obverse
- 1954-S/D Overmintmark
- 1955 Proof Tripled Die Reverse
- 1955-D/S Overmintmark (several dies)
- 1960 Proof Tripled Die Reverse
- 1971 Proof (No "S")

The Jefferson nickel is an excellent series for the new collector because (1) it is affordable, even in Mint State; (2) it offers a challenge (in tracking down Full Steps); (3) quantities are available for every date; and (4) the proliferation of varieties creates tremendous interest.

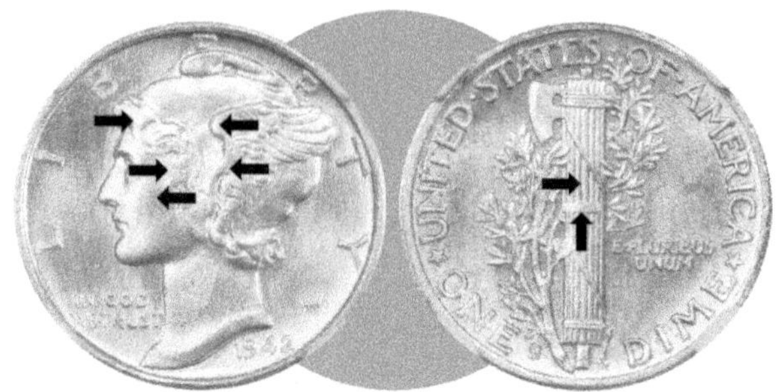

# Grading Hints for the Mercury Dime (1916–1945)

For the Mercury dime, the key areas to check for determining wear are the cheek and the portion of the wing over the ear on the obverse, and the long vertical center stick of the fasces on the reverse.

It is extremely important to check the broad cheek area very closely using the T-n-T method under the proper lighting. In this case again, the rule, rather than the exception, is that "there *are* hairlines or slide marks on the cheek, so go find 'em!" Be sure that you do not neglect this inspection! Very often they are hidden or barely noticeable, but the grading services *will take points off* for these hairline marks and will downgrade an otherwise lovely coin if they find them.

The "bands" referred to when speaking of "Full" or "Full Split" bands are the two center horizontal bands on the reverse. Photos of Full (Full Split), Split, and Non-split bands are included for reference. To be considered "Full," the center bands must show a complete, deep separation between those two bands, and the bands themselves must be raised and rounded (like the McDonald's arches) from the side. "Split" bands still must have the complete separation with no bridges where they merge, but the two bands are flatter, not raised and rounded. "Non-split" bands show one or more bridges and do not have the full separation. The major grading services do not designate "Full (Full Split)" or "Split" bands descriptively on their holders; they will use the abbreviation FB, though, for the top-tier, full-and-raised condition.

Complete, deep separation, with bands well raised.

Complete separation, with flatter bands.

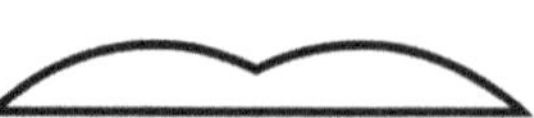

Separation not complete, with one or more "bridges."

Full Split

Split

Non-Split

Some issues (the 1939-S and 1945-P, for example) will very seldom have high, rounded bands. Some leeway is given these dates, but they must still have the full separation (no breaks) to qualify as Full Bands.

Collectors should be conscious of the fact that some of the issues that are difficult to find with full or even split bands, especially the 1945-P, sometimes are altered by cutting a groove in non-split band pieces to "create" a Full Band coin. Inspect the center bands carefully whenever that designation is offered.

*Suggested definitions for Mint State grades:*

**MS-65:** A coin exhibiting attractive, full, natural luster, with no wear and a minimum of contact marks, none detracting. No hairlines on the cheek. The coin may have (natural) toning, but the original luster must still be present. The strike should be full or nearly so for the date, with no detracting weak areas near the rim(s). **Note:** Generally speaking, in order to achieve a higher grade, the coin should also have exceptionally attractive natural toning, as most of the grading services will bump such a piece at least half a grade to a full grade because of the eye appeal.

**MS-64:** A coin with the above characteristics, though it may have some peripheral striking weakness, a few more contact marks, or subdued luster. Still, a very attractive coin. Remember that because of its size, contact/bag marks on a dime are of more consequence, especially on the face, the prime focal area. The coin may have very minor hairlines, but they should be very difficult to detect.

**MS-63:** As in other series, coins falling into this grade usually have more obvious contact or slide marks or hairlines, less or slightly impaired luster, and/or may be weakly struck or produced from worn dies.

**MS-60:** No wear on the wing feathers (obverse) or on the center vertical rod of the fasces (reverse). Luster may be lacking or completely absent (possibly from overdipping). There may be obvious contact marks (especially on the obverse), and the strike may be lacking, even to the point that some of the letters or numbers around the rim(s) are almost missing. May have excessive hairlines.

As on several other series, many of the issues from the late teens and early- to mid-twenties suffer from inadequate striking pressure. Again, this must be factored in when assigning a grade.

In the majority of the Mercuries, the lower of the two center-cross bands is better struck, with the upper band shallower and closer to the level of the sticks in the fasces.

# Grading Hints for the Roosevelt Dime (1946–present)

This series is a "kissin' cuzin" to the Jefferson nickel in many respects, with many features making it particularly collectible:

- All coins are readily available in Mint State.
- They are all inexpensive, even in Mint State.
- There are some important varieties.

Like the Jefferson nickel, there is relatively little interest in specimens that are not Uncirculated. Virtually all the coins dated between 1946 and 1964—minted in silver—sell for "melt price" in Circulated condition, except for a few varieties. The important areas to look at when grading this series are

- **Obverse:** The cheek and the hair above the temple.
- **Reverse:** The outer edges of the leaves and the torch flame.

**Note:** Most grading services now designate "Full Torch Bands" or "Full Bands" for those specimens that show rounded bands, especially the two bottom bands.

As with all coins, luster is all-important in this series. Strike and contact marks, because of its size, are relegated to a lesser position in the grading formula, as most are fairly well struck and devoid of any large, detracting marks. Tip-n-turn the coin to try to pick up any hairlines on the prime focal areas (the face). Remember, this is another portrait coin, and as such, it is susceptible to those slide marks from acetate slides, albums, or improper handling.

There are several particularly important varieties known in this series:

- 1947-S/D Overmintmark (two different dies)
- 1950-S/D Overmintmark
- 1950-D Doubled Die Reverse

- 1963 Proof Doubled Die Reverse (several dies, with one very strong)
- 1968 Proof (No S mintmark)
- 1970 Proof (No S mintmark)
- 1971 Proof (No S mintmark)
- 1983 Proof (No S mintmark)

There are also many other nice doubled dies and repunched mintmarks that command solid premiums in the variety market.

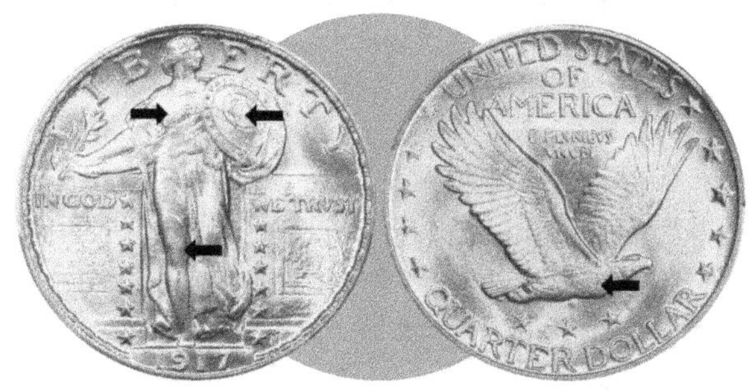


# Grading Hints for the Standing Liberty Quarter (1916–1930)

Experts suggest with this series that you begin by checking the obverse for grading, confirming your opinion afterward by examining the eagle's breast on the reverse. The key area to check to determine wear on this coin is Liberty's knee and (to a lesser degree) the breast and shield.

As on the Buffalo nickel, if the knee area shows a "mesa effect" (like on the buffalo's hip), the coin is not Mint State. Look for a dullness or difference in color in this area as well, which indicates the loss of original luster.

The special designation for this series (in coins minted after 1917) is for Liberty to have a "Full Head." In order to be classified a Full Head, the coin must meet three criteria:

Rounded knee (no wear)

1. The three leaves must be visible on the head,
2. The "ear hole" depression must be visible, and—most important—
3. There must be a complete, unbroken hairline from the forehead to the jaw.

"Mesa Effect" (wear)

*Suggested definitions for Mint State grades:*

**MS-65:** The coin should exhibit attractive, full, natural luster, with no wear and a minimum of contact marks, none detracting. The coin may have (natural) toning, but the original luster must be present. The strike should be full, or nearly so, for the date.

**MS-64:** A coin with the above characteristics, except that it may have subdued luster, a few more obvious contact marks, or exhibit

Full Head

some striking weakness. **Note:** While contact marks are always important in the grading formula, they are less of a consideration on this series because of how busy the design is, especially on the "money side" obverse. Often these marks are hidden in the design and therefore less visible than the same mark on the cheek of a coin with a portrait design such as the Barber series or the Morgan dollar.

**MS-63:** A coin in this mid-Mint State condition will have less or slightly impaired luster, more obvious contact marks, less definition due to a weak strike or having been struck from worn dies, or a combination of the above.

**MS-60:** No wear on the high points, especially Liberty's knee, breast, or shield (particularly check for the mesa effect on the knee). Original luster may be lacking or completely absent due to overdipping. There may also be obvious contact marks, and the strike may be inadequate so that much of the design is ill-defined.

The Type 1 issues (dated 1916 and 1917) have a different design, and the first strikes in 1917 usually display a full head. The criteria listed for a "Full Head" above do not apply for the Type 1 issues. Some of the branch mint coins from the mid-twenties in this series, such as the 1924-D, are extremely difficult to find with this desirable feature.

# Grading Hints for the Washington Quarter (1932–2025)

In my opinion, the Washington quarter is a genuine sleeper in the field of numismatic collecting. Long relatively ignored and rather a neglected stepchild compared to other contemporary series (such as the Lincoln cent, Buffalo nickel, Mercury dime, and Walking Liberty half), this stately nonagenarian offers a great opportunity for contrarians—those who collect coins currently out of favor or relatively price-dormant.

As in most of the other recent coinage, collectors by-and-large gravitate to Uncirculated specimens, leaving all but two or three (the 1932-D and S and the 1936-D) of the Circulated silver issues minted through 1964 for the melting pot (the varieties listed below are an exception). This can only enhance the potential of this series in the future.

The Washington quarter has had several design changes in recent decades. As a result, the first points to show wear depend on the year of minting:

- **Obverse:** Pre-2022, the cheek, the hair over and behind the ear, and the leading edge of the hair at the temple were the highest points of the design. From 2022 to 2025, Washington's portrait on the obverse was updated to the right-facing design originally created by Laura Gardin Fraser in 1931 (as part of the American Women Quarters Program); for these quarters, wear shows first on the high-relief areas of the hair (specifically over the ear and at the temple), the cheekbone, and the tip of the shoulder.
- **Reverse:** Through 1998, the eagle's breast and upper legs and the upper edges of the wings will be the first to show wear. Since 1999 the US Mint has done a variety of special reverses honoring each state, the national parks, and innovative women, and the 250th anniversary of the Declaration of Independence. Each design has its own points that will indicate wear, so focus on the obverse when inspecting more recent coins.

A difference in color—where have we heard this before?—is paramount in detecting wear on these high points. It usually appears as a lighter or darker color compared to the rest of the surrounding design. Again, check carefully for the dreaded hairlines or slidemarks on the face of this portrait coin—remember that grading services are highly critical of them, so make certain if they're there you find them before you buy the coin.

Not unlike every other series, as this coin becomes more worn, the color changes will expand beyond the above areas and also will lose design detail, becoming flatter.

Many serious variety collectors feel that the Washington quarter affords more collectible doubled dies and repunched mintmarks than any other recent series (with the possible exception of the Lincoln cent).

Some of the more important ones are

- 1932-P Doubled Die Obverse
- 1934-P Doubled Die Obverse
- 1934-D Small D (Type used in 1932)
- 1936-P Doubled Die Obverse
- 1937-P Doubled Die Obverse
- 1942-P Doubled Die Reverse
- 1942-D Doubled Die Obverse
- 1942-D Doubled Die Reverse
- 1943-P Doubled Die Obverse (strong)
- 1943-S Doubled Die Obverse
- 1950-D/S Overmintmark
- 1950-S/D Overmintmark
- 1976-D Doubled Die Obverse

You might want to take a serious look at the Washington quarter as your next collecting arena. It offers something for everyone, and one thing's for sure: the price is right!

Please refer to Chapter 11 on weak strikes to learn those in this series that are not usually fully struck up, and to Chapter 14 for reference books on this coin.

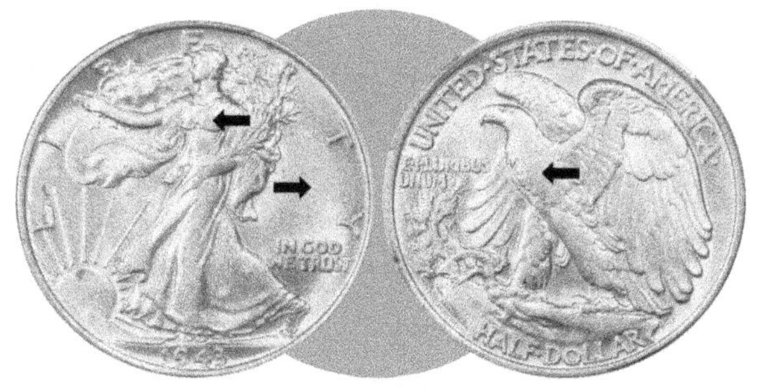

# Grading Hints for the Walking Liberty Half Dollar (1916–1947)

As on the Buffalo nickel, I prefer to grade the Walking Liberty half dollar by examining the reverse first. If there is wear on the reverse in this area, there should be wear on the obverse. The key areas to look at to determine wear are

- **Obverse:** Liberty's breast and the open field behind Liberty.
- **Reverse:** the eagle's breast.

A difference in color on the breast, denoting the loss of original luster, is an indication of wear. If the feathers on the eagle's breast just below the long neck feathers show the dreaded dullness of color change, it cannot be a Mint State coin. However, if this area is shiny, as in the case of the hipbone on the Buffalo nickel, it is likely coin-against-coin damage from being in a roll. Suspected wear may usually be confirmed on the obverse by checking the right field (behind Liberty) for dullness caused by wear disturbing the original luster.

Collectors should be aware that there are many issues in this series (especially the S-mintmarked coins from the 1940s) that are weakly struck. There is often little or no detail on the obverse from the hand down the skirt covering the leg and on the reverse from the eagle's breast down the leg. This can be distinguished from wear because those areas will still show the planchet frost or luster rather than the dull color associated with wear.

*Suggested definitions for Mint State grades:*

**MS-65:** A coin exhibiting attractive, full, natural luster, with no wear and a minimum of contact marks, none detracting. The coin may have natural toning, but the original luster must be present. The strike must be full (or nearly so) for the date.

**MS-64:** A coin with the above characteristics, except that it may have somewhat subdued luster, a few more contact marks in the focal area(s), or a weaker strike.

**MS-63:** Usually a lack of luster and/or a weak strike will determine if a coin receives this grade. It could also have more than its share of contact marks.

**MS-60:** There must be no dullness in the right obverse field or wear on Liberty's breast or especially on the eagle's breast on the reverse, though there may be poor or no original luster (usually due to overdipping). Contact marks usually appear most noticeably in the right field or on the sun on the obverse and throughout the eagle's wing feathers on the reverse. A poor strike will lessen the grade, but the date and mintmark should be factored in to a certain degree.

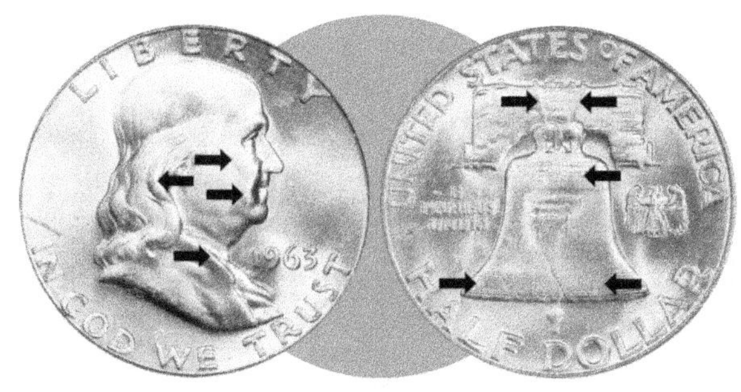


## Grading Hints for the Franklin Half Dollar (1948–1963)

This series, because of the relatively low relief of the obverse and reverse designs, is a bit more difficult to grade than those coins with effigies higher off the field. Minted for only sixteen years (1948–1963), the Franklin half had noticeable striking problems from about 1949 to 1955. Inadequate striking pressure coupled with the use of the dies far beyond their effectiveness created some mushy, ill-defined mintages, especially from the San Francisco Mint during these years (no coins were struck at this facility in 1950 or 1955). This further complicates the problem of properly grading this series.

A full strike will usually produce "Full Bell Lines" on the reverse Liberty Bell, as well as the three wisps of hair in front of Franklin's ear on the obverse. Coins designated as "FBL" should have six complete, unbroken incused lines at the bottom of the bell. Collectors should be aware that the lower set of horizontal lines across the bottom portion of the bell do not continue all the way to the crack. To qualify as an FBL, these lines should extend to within 1/16" of the crack. Issues such as the 1953-S and 1954-S are genuinely rare in MS-65 with full bell lines.

The first points of wear on this coin are

- **Obverse:** The cheek, shoulder, and sweep of hair behind the ear, as well as Franklin's eyebrow.
- **Reverse:** The inscription on the top of the bell ("Pass and Stow"), and the straps around the beam and the lower portion of the bell.

Luster is a critical element in grading any coin, and it is especially so on the Franklin half. Dull, unattractive luster will not garner a high Mint State grade from the grading services, no matter how few contact marks there are. Also, as this is another portrait design, one must check carefully for slide marks or hairlines on the face, as well as on the open area of the bell on the reverse.

This is another series that is not difficult to complete in high Uncirculated condition. As with the Roosevelt dime and JFK half, there are only one or two dates that command a premium much over "melt" (based on the silver market value) in Circulated condition, so it is recommended that you consider only Mint State specimens if you decide to collect this series.

Many attractively toned coins may be found in the government-issued Mint Sets from 1948 to 1958. If especially pleasing, the toning will enhance the chance of obtaining a higher grade from the grading services because of that all-important factor: eye appeal.

# Grading Hints for the Kennedy Half Dollar (1964–present)

For most advanced collectors, the Kennedy half dollar falls into the "W.C." category: "Who Cares?" However, for beginners or those special collectors who delve into nice die varieties, it is a series worth looking at.

As with other half dollars, the Kennedy half is a relatively large coin, and one that is easily collected in Mint State. There are no "stoppers" (expensive coins) in the set, and the majority of the dates are of the clad (copper-nickel exterior bonded to a copper core) composition. The major negative in putting this set together is that they are seldom found in circulation and must be purchased from coin dealers or (for newer issues) directly from the US Mint. This translates into paying some sort of premium for every coin, but usually that premium is very reasonable, and a complete Uncirculated set may be put together with little difficulty and minimal cost.

As in the case of the Jefferson nickel and Roosevelt dime, specimens other than Mint State or Proof fall by the wayside. Even the few business-strikes varieties go begging unless they are Uncirculated. To distinguish a Circulated specimen from a Mint State coin, look at

- **Obverse:** The cheek and jaw, the hair below the part, and the bottom of the bust.
- **Reverse:** The arrows, eagle's neck, center tailfeather, and the right wingtip.

This is a portrait coin—check the prime focal area (the cheek) for those hairlines! Our old friend, the change in color, shows up first on the cheekbone and in the hair just below JFK's part.

There are quite a few doubled die obverses in this series, most notably on the 1964-P and 1964-D (the latter also has a nice Tripled Obverse die). The first year of issue (1964) is the only year this series was issued in 90% silver. Several Proof doubled dies are known, and a strong one may also be found on the clad 1974-D in some Mint sets.

## Grading Hints for the Morgan Dollar (1878–1921)

The Morgan dollar is one of the most popular coins collected today, primarily because it has so many things going for it. It has an attractive, well-balanced design. It is a large coin, made of 90% silver (a precious metal). It has a background rich in the history of this country. And because of the millions of coins produced at five different branch mints, specimens are available in just about any condition.

Weak strikes, especially on many of the New Orleans Mint issues, contribute to some grading difficulties in this series, so please refer to Chapter 11 for a list of which coins often fall into this category.

The first areas to look at to determine wear on this coin are

- **Obverse:** The hair over Liberty's ear, the cheek, the hair under LIBERTY, the outside edges of the leaves on the bonnet, and the cotton balls.
- **Reverse:** The eagle's breast feathers.

Another portrait coin. So what's the prime focal point? Right! Liberty's cheek. Check for hairlines and a loss of luster here and in the hair over the ear and under LIBERTY. If it shows a different color, we have . . . wear! You can usually confirm this by checking the field in front of Liberty where you're most likely to find additional loss of luster and several small "chicken scratch" marks. On the reverse, the eagle's breast is the first area to show the color difference. You may find it helpful to tip the coin away from you when looking for this color change, as it redirects the light for better viewing.

If a Morgan dollar was struck from worn dies or with inadequate striking pressure, the last areas to strike up (the deepest parts of the die) are the same areas where you first encounter wear, which can cause some confusion at times. The thing to remember is that if these flat areas are the result of a weak strike, they should still exhibit the original frosty planchet luster, not the lighter or darker color associated with wear. It takes experience to learn the difference, but with some time and looking at a lot of coins, you'll soon develop the knack of recognizing this characteristic.

# Grading Hints for the Peace Dollar (1921–1935)

Like the Franklin half, the Peace dollar has a low-relief design, making it somewhat difficult to grade. The first year of issue, 1921, had the design a good deal higher, but the Mint soon discovered that this led to several problems—primarily a noticeable weakness of detail when struck. To rectify this, the obverse and reverse designs were modified for 1922 and later by lowering the design features so that they were closer to the field.

While the "money side" is still the obverse, with the large cheek area and its vulnerability to contact marks and wear, the reverse is also very important in determining the grade. The Peace dollar was one of the few series in US coinage that used the reverse die as the hammer (upper) die in the striking process. Because of this, after the coins were struck, they had a tendency to travel down the chute into the collection hopper reverse-side-up, making that side more susceptible to contact marks from other coins falling on top of them. Quite often this series has as many or more contact marks on the reverse as it does on the obverse.

The first points to check to determine wear on this coin are

- **Obverse:** The cheek and neck, the field in front of Liberty, high points of Liberty's hair.
- **Reverse:** The outside edge of the eagle's right wing and the feathers across the eagle's back.

The dullness in color due to wear will be the most obvious on the high points of the hair and cheek on the obverse and the feathers on the eagle's back on the reverse. Again, it will be easier to see this wear (usually visualized by a lighter color) if you tip the coin away from you while looking at these areas through a loupe.

Strike is especially important on several San Francisco Mint issues, particularly the 1923-S, 1924-S, 1925-S, 1927-S, and 1928-S. Well struck, lustrous, minimally marked specimens of these dates command very high prices in MS-65 grade.

The majority of the coins in this series bring only modest premiums in Circulated grades.

More details on weak strikes for this series can be found in Chapter 11.

# Understanding AU-58 and the Nuances of Coin Grading

by David Crenshaw (July 16, 2025)

Bill Fivaz, a respected voice in the world of numismatics, has long championed the importance of discernment in coin grading, particularly concerning the much-debated grade AU-58. In three previously published articles—"AU-58: The Grade of the Future?," "Almost Unlimited Bargains in AU," and "It's Confession and Revelation Time!"—Fivaz presents a cohesive argument for recognizing quality in every grade, challenging traditional assumptions about what collectors should prioritize. While each article contributes uniquely to this discourse, together they paint a comprehensive picture of how grading standards and market perceptions evolve—and why AU-58 coins deserve a closer look.

## AU-58: A Misunderstood Sweet Spot

In "AU-58: The Grade of the Future?," Fivaz first introduced the idea that About Uncirculated (AU) coins—particularly those at the upper end of the range—are often undervalued, despite offering superior eye appeal when compared to many lower Mint State coins. He argues that a properly graded AU-58 coin can appear nearly identical to an MS-64 or MS-65 at first glance, with full luster and minimal marks, only revealing slight wear on the high points upon close inspection. Fivaz dismisses the common misconception that AU-58 coins are merely MS-60s with some wear; rather, he emphasizes that many MS-60s are less desirable due to excessive contact marks or impaired luster.

Fivaz's forward-looking tone is unmistakable. He predicted—correctly, as time has proven—that high-quality AU coins would gain in popularity and market value. His central claim: AU-58 coins offer unmatched value and eye appeal at a fraction of the cost of higher Mint State coins.

## Almost Unlimited Bargains: A Call for Rethinking Priorities

More than two decades later, "Almost Unlimited Bargains in AU" expanded on this idea with greater urgency and clarity. Fivaz revisited the debate from a market-aware perspective, noting that the explosive demand for high-grade MS coins has rendered many of them prohibitively expensive or unattractive due to quality compromises, using vivid metaphors to criticize the often disappointing appearance of MS-60 coins—comparing some to worn-out dogs or overly polished bumpers on vintage cars.

In this article, Fivaz reinforces his belief that quality exists in every grade and asserts that a top-end AU-58 or AU-55 is often far more collectible than a low-end MS-60. He also warns collectors against blindly adhering to the "MS-65 or nothing" mentality. The real challenge, he notes, lies in locating *accurately graded* AU coins—a task made difficult by market pressures and grading inconsistencies. Nonetheless, the opportunity is ripe for collectors who shift their mindset: attractive AU coins are not compromises—they are smart, strategic acquisitions.

## Confession and Revelation: Embracing Grading Complexity

Fivaz took a more introspective turn in "It's Confession and Revelation Time!," reflecting on the evolution of grading systems themselves. Once skeptical of the 11-point Mint State scale, he concedes that nuanced, incremental grading is not only possible but necessary—provided the grader has ample experience and a discerning eye. He illustrates this with a hypothetical scenario: opening a bag of Uncirculated Morgan dollars and naturally sorting them into at least eleven piles, each slightly better or worse than the next. This underscores his argument that grading is not binary but exists on a continuum of quality within each grade.

The article introduces a powerful framework with the idea of "low-end," "mid-grade," and "high-end" coins within the same grade. For collectors, the takeaway is simple: aim for the high end of any grade, including AU-58. This reinforces the assertions of the previous two articles—namely, that market prices alone don't always reflect true quality, and visual appeal is a key factor in collectability.

## Shared Themes and Key Contrasts

Across all three articles, Fivaz advances a central thesis: collectors should prioritize visual quality and overall appeal over strict numeric grade labels. The idea that "there is quality in every grade" threads consistently through each piece, as does his criticism of market tendencies that overvalue numerical grade while undervaluing appearance and honest wear.

However, the articles differ in tone and approach:

- "AU-58: The Grade of the Future?," first printed in 1986, is predictive and somewhat idealistic, written as it was at a time when the numismatic community was just beginning to reconsider AU coins.
- "Almost Unlimited Bargains in AU," printed in 2013, is practical and market-driven, providing updated evidence and a more forceful call to action.

- "It's Confession and Revelation Time!," from 2020, is reflective and systemic, offering a conceptual framework for understanding why grading granularity matters and how quality can be found even within tight numerical bounds.

This trio of writings presents a compelling and consistent case for reevaluating the numismatic community's biases against AU-graded coins, particularly the often-overlooked AU-58. Through a blend of anecdote, market analysis, and grading theory, Fivaz urges collectors to look beyond the label—to judge coins on their true merits. As the coin market continues to evolve, his insights remain not just relevant, but essential for any serious collector aiming to build a collection of lasting value and visual harmony.

## AU-58: The Grade of the Future?

Have you been just a wee bit confused as to why one particular coin in a certain grade sells for a great deal more than another coin of the same date in the same grade? Why does one MS-65 1882-O Morgan dollar, for example, sell for $650 while another, also a legitimate MS-65 specimen, may bring only $400?

While both of these coins might technically grade MS-65, the specimen that garners the higher price probably has that "something" extra in the way of toning and appearance—eye appeal! No two coins are exactly alike (a nick here, an abrasion there); each must stand on its own merit and therefore may command a higher (or lower) price than the one "listed" for that grade.

The point is that there are MS-65s and there are *MS-65s*, just the same as there are coins of different qualities in the grades of MS-63, or even Fine (F), Extremely Fine (EF), and, most important in my opinion, About Uncirculated (AU).

The quality grade in the AU range is *at least* AU-55 and especially AU-58. So that we know what an AU-58 coin really is and what it actually looks like, let's define it. I suggest the following: "AU-58—a coin that when first observed, appears to grade MS-64 or MS-65 (good luster, few contact marks), but on closer examination reveals slight wear on the highest points."

A common misconception is that a high-quality AU-58 "super slider" is just a hair below an MS-60. Nope! Mint State and Circulated coins are graded as separate entities. In reality, AU-58 is much closer to MS-64 or MS-65, with just a touch of honest wear. It jumps right over the MS-60 grade because of what makes an MS-60 an MS-60—lots of contact marks, impaired luster, and, in general, no real eye appeal. Add the same amount of honest wear to a coin such as this and you have an AU-*50*.

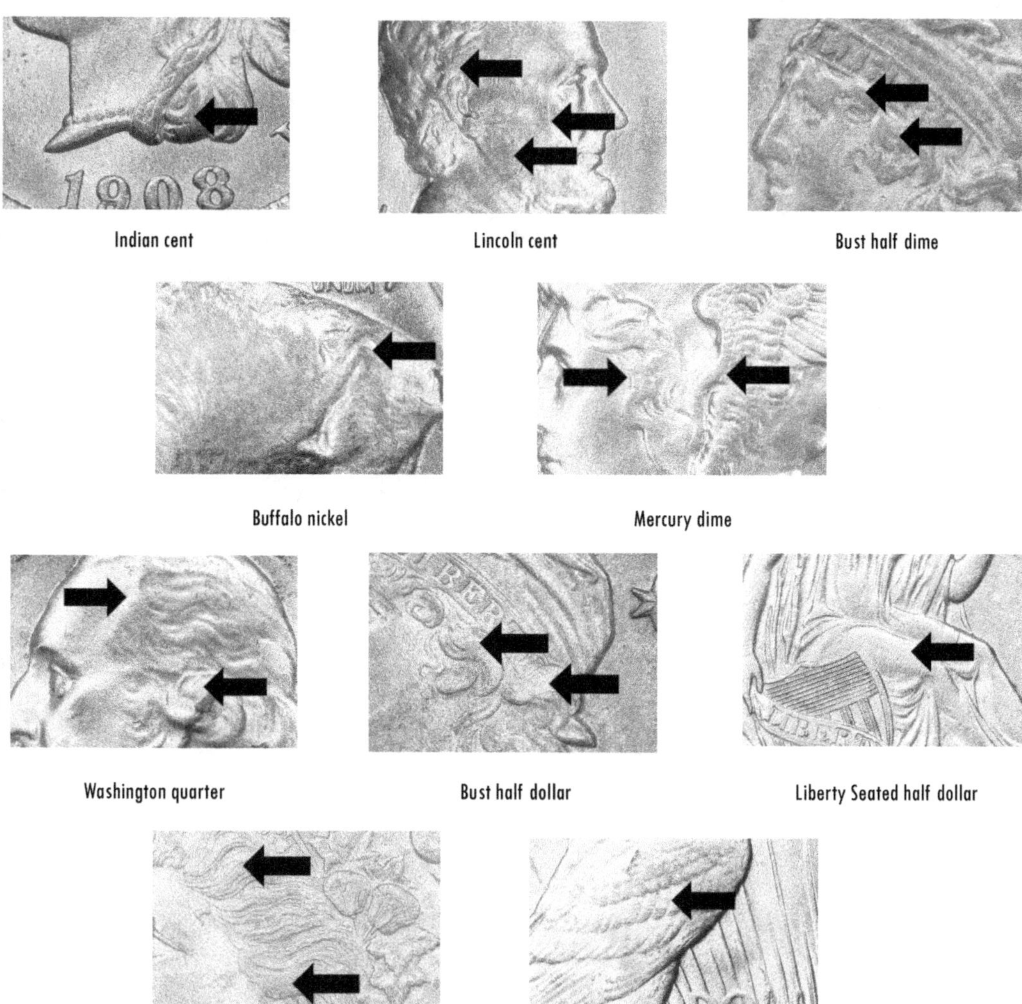


Indian cent

Lincoln cent

Bust half dime

Buffalo nickel

Mercury dime

Washington quarter

Bust half dollar

Liberty Seated half dollar

Morgan dollar

Peace dollar

## Is AU-58 the Grade of the Future?

Why not? Prices for MS-64 and MS-65 coins (and soon MS-63) have, for the most part, skyrocketed into the stratosphere, and properly graded, very choice AU pieces are currently the bargains of the century!

Think about it: top quality AU-graded pieces are much more attractive and priced far less than MS-60s. Someday someone is going to see the light and realize that many (if not most) AU-58s, and even some AU-55s should command a price in excess of MS-60 listings! I don't know when this will happen* but believe me, they're worth it. Don't hesitate to pay a hefty premium for a nice, visually appealing Choice AU coin—in the years ahead you'll be glad you did.

Learn the first points of wear on your series and on some of the popular issues. Look for a loss of detail from wear in these areas, as well as a difference in color (usually dull and flat in the same high areas). Remember, an AU-58 coin must have MS-64 or MS-65 luster and a corresponding lack of marks, with the exception of just that little bit of wear.

If you can locate these properly graded coins at an AU price, grab them—especially type coins and pre-1935 modern issues. Common sense dictates that these are the coins of the future—the ones collectors will seek to complete their sets without having to pay big bucks for the MS-63s, 64s, and 65s.

*This article was written for *The Numismatist* in 1986, and this prediction has come to pass. Many technically AU-58 coins now reside in MS-61 and MS-62 holders, as this is the price they are commanding in the market.

Walking Liberty half dollar (Left) MS-60: No wear, but much of the original luster is gone, with many contact marks in the right field. (Right) AU-58: Nice original luster; just a touch of wear on the breast and leg, with minimal contact marks in field.

## Almost Unlimited Bargains in AU

"Naw, I don't wanna look at any Circulated coins; show me what you've got in Uncirculated!"

At the risk of sounding vain, this article could be one of the most important you've read in some time. I hope it will get you thinking along a slightly different line in your collecting. Whether you act on it is entirely up to you, but I wouldn't tarry too long—it might just pass you by.

Years ago, collectors weren't overly concerned if a "nice-looking" coin had a bit of rub here or there or wasn't truly Uncirculated. If it had nice, original luster and "looked new," it was generally purchased as such and added to the collection. The price differences back then (the 1950s–1980s) weren't nearly as dramatic as they are today, with thousands of dollars often separating AU-58, MS-60, MS-63, and especially MS-64 and MS-65 grades for many coins.

Everyone knows that the current frantic, almost compulsive quest for "quality" has caused Gem material to virtually disappear from the marketplace. The coins that remain are, by and large, pieces with some sort of problem: a noticeable abrasion here, a contact mark on the cheek there, or lackluster sheen. In other words, a bushel of these little round things with the "uglies" would, if they could speak, probably emit a friendly "Bow-wow," wag their tails, and fetch your slippers.

Let's analyze: What makes an MS-60 coin an MS-60? Simply put, it's not very attractive for one reason or another. Many legitimate MS-60 coins, with no wear whatsoever, are still so chewed up they look like they took a 500-mile ride in the back of a gravel truck. Others are dull or dirty-looking, feature edge bumps, or have been cleaned to the point where silver coins resemble the front bumper of a '57 Chevy and copper coins could double as a backdrop for Judy Garland singing "Somewhere Over the Rainbow." Although technically Mint State, these "woofers" rarely sell for anywhere near the MS-60 price to knowledgeable collectors or dealers and often don't even garner an AU quote.

Aha! This should tell us something—if we're listening! *There is quality in every grade!* There are quality Very Fine specimens, just as there are quality Uncirculated coins. There are quality Very Good pieces, just as there are quality AU examples. In the vast majority of cases, a nice, high-end AU coin is far superior in quality and "collectability" to the average MS-60 coin. There are exceptions, but do an honest comparison of a lustrous, properly graded AU-55 or AU-58 Morgan or Peace dollar to an MS-60 example. Which would you most want to add to your collection to keep it as uniform as possible? Probably the AU coin. And after checking the price difference between AU and MS-60 listings? Definitely the AU! There's no glory in having "all Mint State" coins in your collection if many of them (the MS-60s) detract from the others in the set.

An accurately graded AU-55 or AU-58 coin is still very attractive and is generally free of the "problems" that make an MS-60 an MS-60. The only thing it should have to mark it "down" is good, honest wear—and just a little bit of that.

| Year | Denomination | AU | MS-60 | MS-65 |
|---|---|---|---|---|
| 1885 | 1c | $62 | $78 | $500 |
| 1911-S | 1c | $80 | $145 | $2,175 |
| 1912-S | 5c | $100 | $110 | $4,800 |
| 1914-S | 5c | $120 | $135 | $1,575 |
| 1918-D | 10c | $35 | $80 | $450 (not FB) |
| 1921-P | 10c | $670 | $900 | $2,350 (not FB) |
| 1924-S | 25c | $175 | $235 | $1,150 (not FH) |
| 1935-D | 25c | $95 | $190 | $410 |
| 1941-S | 50c | $23 | $60 | $590 |
| 1943-S | 50c | $17 | $35 | $220 |
| 1883-S | $1 | $100 | $675 | $44,500 |
| 1891-O | $1 | $36 | $175 | $7,100 |

(Important Note: September 2013 *Greysheet* prices, pre-publication) AU—MS grade spreads are comparable to 2026 levels.

The challenge, of course, is locating accurately graded, high-end AU coins. The tendency, even among some grading services, is to push these "almost there" examples into the Mint State category ("because that's the price they'll bring in the market"), even if they are *slightly* circulated. So when you do find accurately graded AU-55s and AU-58s, consider adding them to your collection—or even your stock.

I'm telling you straight out: this will take some reorganization of your mindset. We've been so conditioned to "MS-65 Or Nothing" Syndrome that it can be difficult to bring yourself to buy that AU coin. But down the line—and it's almost upon us now—when AU and EF coins are all most collectors can afford, the nice ones will increase in price and disappear from the scene. In my opinion, upper-end AU coins—especially AU-58s and some AU-55s—should command a higher price than MS-60s. This trend has already started.

As stated earlier, there is quality in every grade. A glance at the chart above, taken from the September 2013 *Greysheet,* highlights some interesting price spreads for AU, MS-60, and MS-65 grades for a few randomly selected coins. The AU prices listed are for AU-50 coins, those at the lower end of the AU scale. If you can capture some solid AU-58 or AU-55 specimens (the quality AU coins) at these prices, grab them. I think you'll be delighted you did in the years ahead.

"Naw, I don't wanna look at your Uncirculated coins; show me what you've got in AU!"

## It's Confession and Revelation Time!

**Confession:** Years ago, when the 11-point Mint State grading scale was adopted, I was not alone in shaking my head and telling anyone who would listen that it was impossible to grade Uncirculated coins in one-point increments. How in the world could someone, even the seasoned third-party grading experts, be astute enough to tell an MS-63 from an MS-64 or an MS-64 from an MS-65, etc., with any degree of consistency? It just couldn't be done!

Computer-grading of coins was touted for a while, but faded into the sunset as quickly as it arrived. It was probably possible to measure two of the four basic components of grading by computer—the severity and location of contact marks on each side, as well as the strength of the strike—but what about the two more important factors, luster and eye appeal? These are both elements that only the human eye can evaluate, and no computer was up to that challenge.

**Revelation:** After a bit of reflection on the 11-point grading concept and trying to keep an open mind, I came to the realization that, armed with sufficient expertise and having viewed a lot of coins, yes, incremental-point Mint State grading is possible.

To illustrate my opinion, let's look at the following scenario:

Let's say that you go down to your local bank, the Wombat Federal Savings and Loan, and ask the head teller to sell you that $1,000 bag of Uncirculated 1886-P Morgan dollars that they've had stored in the back corner of their vault for 140 years. He does, and you haul it home and spread out the 1,000 coins on your dining room table (fully prepared to eat out for the next few nights). I would bet a double struck, off-center Peruvian bottle cap that you would be able to arrange those coins into at least eleven piles, with the first pile being the worst-looking pieces, the next pile being a little bit nicer, and so on.

Then, referring to the first chart, I suggest that you would have (at a minimum) eight piles of coins that could represent the grades of MS-60 to MS-67; we must realistically expect that there would be no MS-68, 69, or 70 coins in the bag.

| MS-60 | | | MS-61 | | | MS-62 | | | MS-63 | | | MS-64 | | | MS-65 | | | MS-66 | | | MS-67 | | | MS-68 | | |
|---|---|---|---|---|---|---|---|---|---|---|---|---|---|---|---|---|---|---|---|---|---|---|---|---|---|---|
| 100 | | | 100 | | | 200 | | | 448 | | | 120 | | | 25 | | | 5 | | | 2 | | | 0 | | |
| L | M | H | L | M | H | L | M | H | L | M | H | L | M | H | L | M | H | L | M | H | L | M | H | L | M | H |
| | | | | | | | | | | | | | | | | | | | | | | | | | | |

**$1,000 Face Value Bag—1886-P Morgan dollars (All numbers above are +/–)**

The "guesstimates" I have assigned each grade you might find in the bag are just that, and others may disagree, but it's a figure that hopefully will get the point across.

## There Is Quality in Every Grade

The three columns under each grade represent the Low End (L), the Mid-Grade (M) and the High End (H) of that particular grade. Based on this individual grade expansion, you can see that the original eight piles could, theoretically, expand to as many as 24 piles (8×3). You may only have one or two of coins that you feel fall into the MS-66 or 67 category, one a tad better than the other, but the point is, as stated above, there is quality in every grade, and this is reinforced by the second chart:

| MS-63 | | | MS-64 | | | MS-65 | | | MS-66 | | | MS-67 | | |
|---|---|---|---|---|---|---|---|---|---|---|---|---|---|---|
| 448 | | | 120 | | | 25 | | | 5 | | | 2 | | |
| L | M | H | L | M | H | L | M | H | L | M | H | L | M | H |
| | | | | | | 12 | 8 | 5 | | | | | | |

**$1,000 Face Value Bag—1886-P Morgan dollars (All numbers above are +/–)**

This chart zeros in on MS-65 as the subject grade. The 25 coins you might find in the bag of this particular grade are sub-divided into the three categories I mentioned above—Low End, Mid, and High End examples. This sub-division is applicable to every grade, even circulated grades, and the goal of the collector should be to try to purchase specimens in the third column, those that are at the upper end of the grade—whatever that grade may be.

By virtue of the above, you can see that it is theoretically possible to have between 18 and 24 piles of different quality Uncirculated dollars in an original bag. The key, of course, is grading with consistency. Even professional graders are not completely absolved from mistakes, a fact that they will freely admit, but because they (1) have the years of expertise and (2) look at thousands upon thousands of coins, their accuracy percentage is pretty darn high, and they are certainly capable of grading Mint State coins incrementally.

# Weak Strike Information

Dates in various series are often found weakly struck. A weakly struck coin occurs when the minting process fails to fully transfer the design details from the dies to the planchet due to insufficient pressure, excessive die spacing, or other mechanical issues during striking. This results in coins that exhibit muted, shallow, or incomplete details—particularly in higher-relief areas—rather than the sharp, well-defined features seen on normally struck examples. While weak strikes can sometimes be confused with wear from circulation or worn dies, true weak strikes are minting anomalies that can affect specific dates, mintmarks, or even entire series more or less frequently, making them a notable area of study for collectors interested in error/variety coins or production inconsistencies. This chapter notes dates across various series where weakly struck examples are more commonly encountered.

## Silver and Base Metals

*Indian cents:*

All copper-nickel cents (1859–1864), especially 1863 and 1864; also the 1909-S, to a certain degree.

*Lincoln cents:*

- 1918-S
- 1921-S
- 1922 "No D"**
- 1923-S*
- 1924-S
- 1925-S, D*
- 1926-S
- 1927-S
- 1928-S
- 1929-S
- 1930-S
- 1934-D
- 1935-S

*Buffalo nickel:*

- 1918-D, S
- 1919-D, S*
- 1920-D, S*
- 1921-S
- 1923-S*
- 1925-D, S*
- 1926-D**
- 1927-D, S
- 1928-D, S
- 1929-D, S
- 1930-S
- 1931-S*
- 1934-D*
- 1935-D, S*
- 1937-D 3-Leg

*Mercury dime:*

- 1918-D, S
- 1919-S
- 1920-S
- 1921-P
- 1923-S
- 1924-S
- 1925-D, S
- 1926-D, S
- 1927-D, S
- 1928-S
- 1930-S
- 1931-S
- 1934-P
- 1939-S
- 1944-P
- 1945-P**

*Standing Liberty quarter:*

- 1918-D, S
- 1918/7-S
- 1919-D, S
- 1920-D, S
- 1924-D*, S
- 1926-D, S
- 1927-S*
- 1928-S
- 1929-D

*Washington quarter:*

- 1935-S
- 1940-S
- 1941-S
- 1943-S
- 1944-S

*Walking Liberty half dollar:*

- 1917-S (Obv.)
- 1918-D, S
- 1919-D, S
- 1920-D
- 1921-S
- 1923-S
- 1927-S
- 1928-S
- 1935-D, S
- 1940-S*
- 1941-S*
- 1942-S
- 1944-S*
- 1945-S

*Franklin half dollar:*

- 1949-S
- 1951-S
- 1952-S
- 1953-S*
- 1954-S*

*—coins are seldom found with a good strike
**—coins are almost never found fully struck

We're very grateful to the experts whose knowledge contributed to this list: Hal Kritzman, Gary Sturtridge, David Hall, and John Hunter. And thanks as well for their input to the following list of "often weakly struck" Morgan and Peace dollars. Randy Campbell in particular offers us a very comprehensive analysis for the obverse and reverse strikes of these two important series:

*Key:*

1—Very strong strike
2—Above average strike
3—Average strike
4—Below average strike
5—Very weak strike

*Morgan $1*

| Date | Obv. | Rev. | Comments |
|---|---|---|---|
| 1878 8 TF | 2 | 2 | Tail Feathers. |
| 1878 7/8 TF | 2 | 3 | Tail Feathers. Weakness often found in legs, claws. |
| 1878 7 TF PAF | 2 | 2 | Tail Feathers. Parallel Arrow Feather (Reverse of 1878). |
| 1878 7 TF SAF | 3 | 3 | Tail Feathers. Slanted Arrow Feather (Reverse of 1879). Full strikes are scarce. |
| 1878-CC | 2 | 3 | Legs, claws, arrowheads weak. |
| 1878-S | 1 | 2 | |
| 1879-P | 2 | 3 | Wide range in strike. |
| 1879-O | 2 | 2 | Wear often mistaken for "weak strike." |
| 1879-S PAF | 2 | 2 | Parallel Arrow Feather (Reverse of 1878). |
| 1879-S SAF | 1 | 1 | Slanted Arrow Feather (Reverse of 1879). A few weak strikes in Redfield hoard. |
| 1879-CC | 2 | 3 | |
| 1880-P | 3 | 3 | Somewhat soft in centers. |
| 1880-CC PAF | 2 | 2 | Parallel Arrow Feather (Reverse of 1878). |
| 1880-CC SAF | 4 | 3 | Slanted Arrow Feather (Reverse of 1879). Soft strike over ear. |
| 1880-O | 2 | 3 | See '79-O. |
| 1880-S | 1 | 1 | |
| 1881-P | 3 | 3 | |
| 1881-CC | 1 | 2 | The best struck "CC" dollar. |
| 1881-O | 2 | 2 | |
| 1881-S | 1 | 1 | Best strike in Morgan series. |
| 1882-P | 2 | 2 | |
| 1882-CC | 2 | 3 | |

*Key:*
1—Very strong strike
2—Above average strike
3—Average strike
4—Below average strike
5—Very weak strike

| Date | Obv. | Rev. | Comments |
|---|---|---|---|
| 1882-O | 2 | 4 | Flat breast feathers on many. |
| 1882-O/S | 3 | 4 | Unknown in Gem Full Strike. |
| 1882-S | 2 | 2 | Not as well struck as '80-S and '81-S. |
| 1883-P | 2 | 3 | Flat rev on many Prooflike coins. |
| 1883-CC | 2 | 2 | |
| 1883-O | 3 | 4 | |
| 1883-S | 2 | 2 | |
| 1884-P | 3 | 2 | |
| 1884-CC | 2 | 2 | |
| 1884-O | 3 | 3 | |
| 1884-S | 2 | 2 | |
| 1885-P | 2 | 2 | |
| 1885-CC | 2 | 2 | |
| 1885-O | 3 | 4 | |
| 1885-S | 2 | 3 | |
| 1886-P | 2 | 3 | |
| 1886-O | 2 | 2 | Contrary to popular belief, this date is generally well struck. |
| 1886-S | 2 | 2 | |
| 1887-P | 2 | 2 | |
| 1887-O | 4 | 4 | |
| 1887-S | 2 | 2 | |
| 1888-P | 2 | 2 | |
| 1888-O | 4 | 4 | Only full strikes are worth the full *Greysheet* MS-65 bid price. |
| 1888-S | 2 | 3 | |
| 1889-P | 3 | 3 | Elusive in full strike. |
| 1889-O | 4 | 4 | |
| 1889-S | 2 | 2 | |
| 1890-P | 2 | 3 | Weakness often on eagle. |
| 1890-O | 4 | 4 | |
| 1890-S | 1 | 2 | |

| Date | Obv. | Rev. | Comments |
|---|---|---|---|
| 1890-CC | 2 | 2 | |
| 1891-P | 3 | 3 | Below average for "P" Mint. |
| 1891-CC | 3 | 2 | Often flat above ear. |
| 1891-O | 5 | 5 | Extremely flat rev. |
| 1891-S | 1 | 2 | |
| 1892-P | 3 | 3 | |
| 1892-O | 5 | 5 | Usually terrible! |
| 1892-S | 2 | 2 | |
| 1892-CC | 2 | 3 | |
| 1893-P | 2 | 2 | |
| 1893-CC | 4 | 4 | Poorest of the "CC" issues. |
| 1893-O | 4 | 5 | |
| 1893-S | 2 | 2 | |
| 1894-P | 2 | 3 | |
| 1894-O | 4 | 4 | Unknown in Full Strike Gem BU. |
| 1894-S | 2 | 3 | |
| 1895-O | 3 | 3 | Better struck than generally believed. |
| 1895-S | 2 | 2 | |
| 1896-P | 2 | 2 | |
| 1896-O | 4 | 4 | |
| 1896-S | 3 | 3 | |
| 1897-P | 2 | 2 | |
| 1897-O | 3 | 4 | |
| 1897-S | 2 | 1 | |
| 1898-P | 2 | 2 | |
| 1898-O | 2 | 2 | Wide range in strike. |
| 1898-S | 2 | 2 | |
| 1899-P | 3 | 3 | |
| 1899-O | 2 | 2 | Wide range in strike. |
| 1899-S | 2 | 2 | |
| 1900-P | 3 | 3 | Seldom seen in Full Strike. |
| 1900-O | 2 | 2 | |

*Key:*

1—Very strong strike
2—Above average strike
3—Average strike
4—Below average strike
5—Very weak strike

| Date | Obv. | Rev. | Comments |
|---|---|---|---|
| 1900-O/CC | 2 | 4 | |
| 1900-S | 2 | 3 | |
| 1901-P | 4 | 4 | |
| 1901-O | 4 | 4 | |
| 1901-S | 3 | 4 | |
| 1902-P | 2 | 3 | |
| 1902-O | 4 | 4 | Full Strike Gems are very scarce. |
| 1902-S | 3 | 4 | |
| 1903-P | 2 | 2 | |
| 1903-O | 2 | 3 | |
| 1903-S | 2 | 2 | |
| 1904-P | 3 | 4 | |
| 1904-O | 4 | 4 | |
| 1904-S | 3 | 4 | |
| 1921-P | 3 | 4 | |
| 1921-D | 4 | 4 | |
| 1921-S | 4 | 5 | Worst struck "S"-Mint Morgan. |

*Peace $1:*

| Date | Obv. | Rev. | Comments |
|---|---|---|---|
| 1921 | 4 | 4 | Very tough coin to grade. |
| 1922-P | 2 | 3 | |
| 1922-D | 3 | 3 | |
| 1922-S | 4 | 4 | |
| 1923-P | 2 | 2 | |
| 1923-D | 3 | 3 | |
| 1923-S | 4 | 5 | |
| 1924-P | 2 | 2 | |
| 1924-S | 3 | 3 | |
| 1925-P | 1 | 1 | Best struck Peace $1. |
| 1925-S | 5 | 5 | Worst struck Peace $1. |
| 1926-P | 2 | 2 | |
| 1926-D | 2 | 2 | Best struck "D"-Mint Peace $1. |

| Date | Obv. | Rev. | Comments |
|---|---|---|---|
| 1926-S | 2 | 2 | Best struck "S"-Mint Peace $1. |
| 1927-P | 2 | 2 | |
| 1927-D | 3 | 3 | |
| 1927-S | 3 | 4 | |
| 1928-P | 2 | 3 | |
| 1928-S | 4 | 5 | Reverse often pancake flat. |
| 1934-P | 3 | 3 | |
| 1934-D | 3 | 3 | |
| 1934-S | 4 | 3 | Better struck than most "S" Peace $1. |
| 1935-P | 3 | 3 | |
| 1935-S | 3 | 3 | Second best strike of "S" Peace $1. |

**Tips:** The most undervalued Morgans on a price/rarity ratio are MS-65 Deep Mirror Prooflikes. The most undervalued Peace dollars are better date issues in MS-64, such as the 1923-S; 1925-S; 1927-P, D, and S; and 1928-S. These are still affordable in MS-64 but expensive in MS-65. (per Randy Campbell)

## Gold

Comments on pre-1834 gold pieces would be too varied to include in this analysis. Thanks go to Fred Weinberg for his analysis of strikes for these gold denominations.

*$1 Gold:*

**Type 1 (1849–1854):** Many dates come weakly struck in the hair below LIBERTY and behind the ear. Most Charlotte and Dahlonega pieces of all denominations come weakly struck to *very* weakly struck 98% of the time. The 1849-D is a date that is especially weakly struck.

**Type 2 (1854–1856):** The rule on both 1854 and 1855 (especially the '55) is that the "LL" in DOLLAR and "85" in the date are weakly struck on the reverse. On some specimens the middle digits are virtually non-existent.

**Type 3 (1856–1889):** The 1856 and 1857 are occasionally seen with very weak strikes on the upper half of the coin and can come weakly struck in general. The same also applies to the 1874. Other than these dates, Type 3s are generally well struck.

*$2.50 Liberty (1834–1907):*

The Classic Head series, especially the 1836 and 1837, are softly struck in the center, and aside from the 1838 and 1839, the earlier dates are almost never well struck up in the hair curls. Among the **weak** dates are the 1853, 1856, 1857-S, 1859-S, 1867-S, 1869-S, 1876-S in the earlier series. Most coins in the 1880s, 1890s, and 1900s are **well struck**.

*$2.50 Indian (1908–1929):*

The 1910, 1914-D, and 1925-D almost always come with a weak strike. Although most people think that the 1908 comes weakly struck, the fact is that the reverse die was never prepared with full feathers, and so in contrast to later dates, it appears very soft. Mintmarks are often very weakly struck.

*$3 Gold (1854–1889):*

The 1854 is almost always weak below LIBERTY, even on Mint State specimens. The bow and ribbon on the reverse is also very often weakly struck. Almost all "S"-Mint $3s are weakly struck.

*$4 Stellas (1879–1880):*

These generally come well struck, although many have adjustment marks through the center of the coin.

*$5 Liberty (1834–1908):*

Same comments apply as for the $2.50 Classic Head series. As on the $1 and $2.50 coins, the Charlotte and Dahlonega Mint coins are weakly struck, although somewhat better in this $5 denomination. The dates most commonly found with a weak strike include 1854-O, 1855-O, 1867-S, 1869-S, 1873-CC, 1875-CC, and 1884-CC.

*$5 Indian (1908–1929):*

The 1909-O, 1910-S, 1912-S, and 1915-S are usually encountered with weak strikes. The same comments apply to the $5 Indian as the $2.50 Indian.

*$10 Liberty (1838–1907):*

The following are seen weakly struck at least 50% of the time: most "CC" mintmarks, 1841-O, 1844-O, 1847-O, 1848-O, 1851-O, 1852-O, 1854-O, 1861-S, 1862-S, 1864-S, 1868-S, 1873-S, 1874-S, 1880-S, 1883-S, 1888-S, 1893-S, 1896-S, and 1906-S.

*$10 Indian (1907–1933):*

The 1908-D No Motto and With Motto varieties and almost all of the "S"-Mint's coins—especially the 1910-S and 1920-S—are weakly struck. Because of the design on both dies, even the common dates are not usually fully struck up on the breast feathers.

*$20 Liberty (1849–1907):*

Because of the particularly detailed design on the Liberty $20s, many exhibit weakness on the tailfeathers below the shield. Coins from the Philadelphia Mint that are rarely seen fully struck are the 1878, 1888, 1902, 1905 and 1906. In contrast, the 1894-P generally comes with a nice, full strike. Most the "O"-Mint coins are not so much "weakly struck" as they are not fully struck up. Also, because of the design for Type 1 and Type 2 (minted between 1849 and 1876), there is not as much detail or relief as on a 1904, for example, but again, this is due to die design rather than striking inadequacies.

*$20 St. Gaudens (1907–1933):*

The 1907 and 1908 often come weakly struck, and the 1912-P, 1913-P, 1920-S, 1924-D, and 1927-S are often found not fully struck up. Later dates are not quite as softly struck as the 1907 and 1908.

# The Modern Minting Process

Understanding the minting process is like having a superpower in numismatics—it helps you spot genuine treasures, appreciate varieties, and even hunt for those rare errors that make collecting exciting. A key distinction to grasp upfront is the difference between varieties and errors: varieties arise during the die-making process (such as doubled dies or overdates), resulting from intentional or unintentional changes to the die itself, so that every coin struck from that die will show the same, repeatable characteristic. In contrast, errors are unique planchet or mechanical mishaps during the production of blanks and planchets (clipped planchets) or while striking an individual coin (like off-center strikes or wrong planchets), making them one-of-a-kind rather than repeatable.

In today's US Mint operations, high-tech machines and skilled artists team up to produce billions of coins every year at facilities in Philadelphia, Denver, San Francisco, and West Point. Sadly, true errors are now extremely uncommon thanks to rigorous quality controls, though varieties can still emerge from the die preparation stage.

## Design and Sculpting

Every coin begins as a creative vision. Once the Secretary of the Treasury gives the green light to a new design (often inspired by laws passed by Congress), talented Mint artists get to work. They start with sketches and research—photos, historical references, or even field trips to capture details of their images accurately.

Artists build a 3D model using clay, plaster, or digital tools in a size much larger than the final coin to view the design precisely. This oversized sculpt gets refined until it's perfect and then digitally scanned. The digital file is resized and used to carve the design into steel tools the exact size of the final coins called *hubs*. These hubs create the stamps (*dies*) that will press the image onto your coins. Fun fact: Presently, mintmarks like "P" for Philadelphia or "D" for Denver are added here in the digital stage or early hubbing, ensuring they're part of every coin from the start.

This phase is where some cool varieties can sneak in, like subtle design tweaks from artist revisions. As a beginner, keep an eye out for these—they're repeatable differences that add value to your collection without being one-of-a-kind mistakes.

### Blank Production

The real action kicks off with giant rolls of metal alloy, each about 1,500 feet long and tailored to the coin's needs (like copper-plated zinc for pennies). These coils arrive from suppliers already mixed to the exact composition specifications.

A massive blanking machine straightens the coil and punches out round discs, or *blanks*, like a super-fast cookie cutter—cranking out up to 14,000 blanks per minute! The leftover metal scraps (webbing) get shredded and recycled to keep things eco-friendly. Blanks are a tad larger in diameter than the finished coin, but the same thickness.

For most circulating coins (nickels, dimes, quarters, etc.), the Mint makes its own blanks. Blanks for bullion products, many collector pieces, and the limited remaining collectible cents (such as those for America's 250th Anniversary, Proof sets, and Mint sets) are often supplied pre-made by external vendors, allowing the process to skip straight to later striking and finishing steps. The blanks for these final collector cents are drawn from the Mint's existing inventory following the cessation of circulating cent production in November 2025.

### Preparing Planchets

Blanks are tough and brittle straight from the punch, so they head to an annealing furnace. Heated to around 1,600°F in an oxygen-free chamber (to avoid discoloration), they soften up for shaping. Then, they're quenched in a special water bath with lubricants to cool quickly without sticking.

Next stop: washing! A gentle cleaning solution removes any residue and restores the metal's natural shine. After steam-drying, blanks roll into the upsetting mill. This clever machine squeezes the edges in a narrowing groove, pushing metal upward to form a raised rim. Voilà—a blank becomes a planchet, ready for striking. That rim isn't just for looks; it helps metal flow during pressing, protects the design from wear, and makes coins stack neatly.

**Note:** Special Uncirculated or Proof planchets get extra pampering with burnishing—tumbling in drums with polishing pellets for a mirror-like glow.

### Striking the Design

Planchets hop into high-speed presses (up to 750 strikes per minute per machine). Sandwiched between an obverse die (usually the "heads" side) and reverse die (tails), with a collar holding everything in place, immense pressure—from 35 to over 500 tons—smashes the design onto both sides at once.

- **Circulating coins:** One quick strike for everyday pocket change.
- **Proof coins:** Struck multiple times slowly for sharp details and frosty contrasts.
- **Edges:** The collar adds reeding (those ridges on dimes and quarters) or smooth finishes. Modern dollars can get lettering rolled on separately.

Philadelphia and Denver churn out millions daily—47,000+ coins per minute when all presses are humming! Dies are heat-treated and chrome-plated for durability, each lasting for hundreds of thousands of strikes.

Errors can happen here, like off-center strikes or double impressions. But modern sensors and post-strike screenings catch most before they escape the Mint.

### Quality Check and Packaging

Fresh coins tumble out for inspection. Samples are checked under magnification; duds go to a "waffler" that crimps them to indicate they will be recycled. Good ones get counted, weighed, and bagged in huge sacks for shipment to Federal Reserve Banks, who distribute them to your local bank.

Collector coins? Hand-packaged in protective holders, lenses, or boxes. Bullion ships in secure "monster boxes" to dealers.

### Why This Matters

Knowing these steps turns you into a savvy hunter. Planchet flaws might cause "clipped" edges (errors), die issues lead to doubled details (varieties), and striking mishaps create unique errors like broadstrikes. Start simple—examine your change for anything odd, and remember: the Mint's tech has slashed errors since the 1990s, making survivors rarer and more fun to find.

# Numismatic Terms and Definitions

Every new field comes with its own language, and numismatics—the study and collecting of coins, medals, paper money, and related items—is no exception. Whether you're just starting out or deepening your knowledge, this glossary provides clear definitions of key terms to help you navigate descriptions, catalogs, and conversations with confidence.

## General Numismatic Terms

- **adjustment marks**—file marks inflicted on a planchet before striking to reduce the weight of the coin to the minimum standard. They do not constitute impairment to the coin (unless unusually severe). Seen primarily on gold and silver coins minted from 1794 through the early 1800s.
- **annealing**—the heating and cooling process by which coin blanks, dies, and hubs are softened to allow the metal to be worked.
- **bag marks**—marks on a coin's surface made by contact with other coins, often while sliding around in bags. (Technically speaking, bags themselves do not make marks on coins.)
- **blank**—a disc of metal intended ultimately for coinage. A blank has not yet gone through the upsetting mill to form the raised rims of a planchet.
- **blundered die**—one containing an error in entry of one or more letter or numeral punches; usually associated with grossly misplaced numbers (in the denticles, in the bust, etc.).
- **bourse**—the "selling/buying floor" at a show or convention where dealers present their material for sale.
- **branch mint**—a US mint location other than the main Mint in Philadelphia. Branch mints currently active are Denver (D), San Francisco (S), and West Point (W). Those which have struck coins but are now closed

include Charlotte, NC (C); Carson City, NV (CC); Dahlonega, GA (D); and New Orleans, LA (O).

- **brockage**—when a struck coin remains on either die after being struck and impresses its image into the next blank planchet(s) during striking, leaving a negative or "incuse" image. A "partial brockage" may occur when a struck coin comes between the die and a planchet and is partially impressed into the blank, leaving that portion of its design incused in the newly struck coin. In each case, the struck coin creating the brockage acts as a die and leaves a mirror image on the new coin.
- **bust**—coin design representing the head, neck, and sometimes the shoulder of a person or personification of an idea, such as Liberty.
- **business strike**—a coin produced by only one striking of the dies, intended for general commerce.
- **Cameo**—usually referring to Morgan dollars or Proof coins that display a dramatic contrast between the design (raised portions of the obverse or reverse) and the field, resembling a jewelry cameo.
- **cartwheel effect**—original Mint luster on a business strike coin that creates radial lines in the field, which "walk around the coin" when tipped or turned under light. These lines resemble the spokes of a wheel, thus the name.
- **center dot**—a raised dot at the geometric center of a coin from the compass used on the working die to lay out circular arcs for positioning lettering, stars, dates, or other peripheral elements. Normally seen on half and large cents.
- **Circulated**—a coin that shows wear on the high points from being in commerce and handled during the normal course of business.
- **clad**—a coin composition, such as is seen in the current dime, quarter, or half dollar, produced by bonding two layers of one metal to a core of another metal. The above coins have a copper-nickel exterior bonded to a copper core.
- **clash marks**—marks left in the dies when two dies (an obverse and reverse) come together without a planchet between them; in many cases portions of the designs of these two dies are impressed upon each other. All coins then struck by these affected dies will exhibit these marks until they are polished off, worn away or the die(s) retired.
- **clip**—technically, an incomplete planchet. A coin which has (usually) a rounded area missing from it. The missing area was on the planchet prior to striking and did not occur after the coin was struck.
- **coffin coins**—professionally graded coins encapsulated in plastic holders.
- **collar**—a steel ring used to retain the planchet in the striking chamber and on the lower die during the striking process.

- **countermark**—any letters, numerals, or devices stamped into a finished coin.
- **counterstamp**—a device or design stamped over another coin.
- **cud**—a lump of raised metal on the surface of a coin, created when a portion of the die has broken away, leaving a void. It is not "extra" metal, but rather the metal from the planchet "oozing" into the cavity left from the broken die at the time of striking.
- **denticles or dentils**—a tooth-shaped raised design around the rims of some coins. They may be rectangular, rounded, or with dull points. They are part of the die design.
- **die**—a cylindrical-shaped piece of steel with the intended coin design incused at one end, used to stamp the design into a planchet.
- **device**—the principal design on a coin.
- **die markers**—characteristics such as die gouges or polishing marks, etc. on a coin's surface that were transferred directly from the die. These assist in identifying the variety from other similar coins.
- **die crack, die break**—usually a thin, raised, irregular line on the surface of a coin, almost always leading from some area on the rim toward the center of the coin (crack); a crack often becomes a break when the crack widens enough that planchet metal seeps into it, widening it further. This is often accompanied by a small raised "blob" where a piece of the die has fallen away. A major die break creates a cud.
- **die polishing**—usually exemplified by thin, raised lines on the surface of a coin, almost always occurring in the field and rarely on the raised design. Quite often dies were polished to remove clash marks.
- **die state**—the condition of the die(s) that struck a coin. Fresh (new) dies create a crisp, sharp image, while dies that are worn are exemplified by a deteriorating loss of detail.
- **doubled die**—a variety that occurs when the die that strikes the coin has a doubled image (generally caused by a misplaced strike during hubbing). It is characterized by the secondary image on the coin being raised and rounded, often with distinctive splits in the serifs of the letters or numbers.
- **edge**—the "third side" of a coin, which is often overlooked; it may be plain, reeded, lettered, or ornamented.
- **exergue**—the lower edge of a coin's circular area, generally set off from the remainder by a straight line. It may contain the date (as on the Standing Liberty quarter) or lettering (as on the Buffalo nickel).
- **fasces**—a Roman emblem of an axe with its handle surrounded by a bundle of sticks and bound by thongs. The reverse of the Mercury dime depicts a fasces.
- **field**—the plain, flat area surrounding the devices on a coin. The highest part of a die and the lowest part of a coin.

- **Galvano**—a metal positive replica (usually copper) of an oversized plaster relief model, created by electroplating. It served as the master pattern for mechanical reduction to create original hubs and dies for coins or medals. In the modern minting process, the Galvano has been largely replaced by digital sculpting.
- **hub**—a cylindrical-shaped piece of steel with the intended coin design in relief (raised) on one end, as it would appear on the finished coin. A hub is used to produce dies, which in turn produce coins.
- **incuse/intaglio**—letters or devices on a coin sunk below the neighboring surfaces. Fraser's initial "F" below the date on the Buffalo nickel is an incuse design.
- **Janvier Machine**—a type of machine used in the mint that reduces the design from a large Galvano to a hub, the actual size of a coin. The modern minting process moved away from the Janvier machine to computer numerical control (CNC) milling machines.
- **legend**—a coin's inscription.
- **lettered edge**—edge decoration made of lettering put on a planchet prior to striking by a Castaing machine. Found on US late-eighteenth and early-nineteenth century gold and high denomination silver coins, the St. Gaudens $10 and $20 coins, and some modern dollar coins.
- **logotype**—a single punch containing a word or two to four digits of a date.
- **Mint State**—another term for Uncirculated, or showing no wear.
- **mintmark**—a letter or letters placed on the die to indicate at which Mint the coin was struck. All mintmarks were at one time individually punched into the dies, but recently they have become a part of the master die design.
- **motto**—a phrase on a coin, such as IN GOD WE TRUST or E PLURIBUS UNUM.
- **mule**—the use of two dies on a coin (an obverse and reverse) that were not meant to go together.
- **obverse**—the "heads" side of a coin.
- **overdate**—a variety in which at least one digit of the date has been hubbed over or altered to a different number in the die; may have been unintentional, or an instance of the Mint intentionally reusing a die.
- **overmintmark**—a variety in which one mintmark has been punched over a different letter.
- **overstrike**—to use an already-minted coin as a planchet for another.
- **plain edge**—a coin without reeding, lettering, or ornamentation, as on our current cents and nickels.
- **planchet**—the disc of metal with raised rims (having gone through the upsetting mill) intended to become a coin when struck by dies.

- **planchet striations**—incused lines in the planchet (before striking) from burrs or nicks on the knife blade used to clean the surface of the coinage strip prior to going through the blanking process. These lines should always be parallel and appear most prominently in the areas of high relief on the coin, such as in the area above the hair and ear on the Morgan dollar. Areas of low relief on the coin (field) have generally had these striations obliterated due to the greater striking pressure in these areas.
- **Proof**—a specially minted coin, struck at least twice on specially prepared planchets by specially prepared dies, manufactured primarily for collectors. The design detail on a Proof coin is generally sharper than on a business strike.
- **Rarity Scale**—the estimate of the surviving population of a certain coin, represented in several different ways, the most popular being the R-1 to R-8 scale, with R-1 the most common and R-8 representing the rarest.
- ***Red Book***—book published annually containing the retail value of US coins ("The Bible").
- **reeded edge**—the lines or "ribs" on a coin's edge, as on modern dimes and quarters, produced by the collar at the time of striking.
- **relief**—the part of a coin's design above the surface (field) of the coin, such as the lettering, main device, etc. The opposite of incuse.
- **repunched date**—a date or portion thereof, which has been punched in addition to the regular punch, generally in a different position or location. See also "overdate."
- **repunched mintmark**—a mintmark that has been punched in addition to the regular punch in a different position or location.
- **reverse**—the "tails" side of a coin.
- **rim**—the area on the obverse and reverse of a coin where the border meets the edge. A part of the obverse and reverse design.
- **rusted die**—deterioration of a die as the result of moisture or humidity, which creates small pits in (usually) the recessed design areas of that die. Typically exemplified by small raised "pimples" on the highest parts of the coin.
- **serif**—a small terminal line across the top or bottom of a main stroke of a letter or number.
- **signature**—initial(s) or name of a designer or engraver included in a coin design.
- **slider**—a coin not of the advertised grade. Often an EF or AU coin that has been cleaned and/or retoned and touted as an "Uncirculated" grade. Close inspection will confirm a bit of wear on the high point(s) of the coin. A coin that can "slide" from one grade to a higher one.

- **Special Mint Sets**—a compensation for the lack of Proof Sets minted during the years 1965 to 1967. These lacked the crisp detail of the Proofs (probably only struck once, but on special planchets).
- **strike (machine) doubling**—an error showing a second, offset duplicate of the coin design, very often confused with and identified as "die doubling." It can be differentiated by the secondary image being flat, shelf-like, and close to the field, not raised and rounded as on a doubled die. This occurs in several ways, the most common being when one die is loose and twists slightly upon striking the planchet, actually shearing the metal off the edges of some letters and/or numbers. Generally speaking, when all the letters/numbers and the mintmark show the same type of "doubling," it is virtually always strike or machine doubling. Until recently, the mintmark was applied to the die after it was made, so it would not be affected if the die was doubled.
- **store card**—any token advertising the issuing firm. Usually small-cent size.
- **truncation**—the lower cutoff edge of a head or bust in a portrait design.
- **type**—a major variance of the basic design, such as the 1913 Buffalo nickels—one featured the bison standing on a mound, and later that year the animal stood on a plain.
- **variety**—a coin different in some way to others of the same type and year. Doubled dies, repunched mintmarks, die breaks, and clashed dies are considered varieties, among others.
- **whizzing**—the deceptive practice of giving a coin a false surface, fraudulently simulating Mint bloom. Usually created by a high-speed wire brush. This process results in various degrees of distortion to the coin's elements upon close inspection, often including metal build up on the outside edges of the letters and/ or numbers.
- **worn die**—die deterioration after prolonged use. Often manifests itself by an "orange peel" quality to the field. The lettering and devices may also become mushy and lack detail in most cases.

## Bourse Floor Jargon

If you thought the general numismatic terms were rough, just wait until you go to your first show and hear the dealers chatting on the bourse floor. You'll probably think that you've just landed in a foreign country or that the floor was rife with extra-terrestrials from the planet Newp. "I just got this rip from a fish and sent it to Slab City, figuring it was a 4-shot-5, but it came back in a body bag as AT." Say what?

Actually, what the guy was saying was, "I just bought this underpriced (or undergraded) coin from someone who really didn't know what he was doing and sent it to one of the grading services, as I thought it was at least a MS-64 and maybe a MS-65, but it came back without a grade, because they felt the toning on the piece was artificial."

Now, I'm not really a dealer, and some of the descriptions below might not be 100% accurate, but they're close enough to give you an idea of what dealers are saying to each other when they converse in this cryptic or even neo-galactic language. I thought I might offer what I believe is a close translation of various terms.

- **3, 4, 5 (etc.)**—shorthand for "MS-63," "MS-64," and "MS-65," etc.
- **AT**—Artificial Toning. Color on a coin that is not natural but rather applied, usually by a chemical process, to make the coin appear more attractive (and therefore, worth more).
- **blast**—extraordinary luster on a coin.
- **blazer**—similar to "blast" but not quite as impressive.
- ***Blue Book***—a book published annually giving guidance to the wholesale values of US coins.
- **body bag**—a coin returned from a third party grading service without a grade because of a problem on the coin (AT, cleaned, severe damage, etc.). It arrives back in a soft plastic flip (the "body bag") with the reason for rejection on it.
- **buried**—the mistake of buying a coin for more than you can readily sell it for.
- **cherrypick**—to purchase a coin with a variety on it (unbeknownst to the seller) for the price of the normal coin. The art of using one's knowledge to purchase a seemingly "normal" coin, but which has something different about it that makes it worth more money than the price of the regular coin. It may be a doubled die, repunched mintmark, or other die variety that was overlooked by the owner. This term may also apply to purchasing an undergraded coin for the lower price.
- **DMPL**—"Deep Mirror Prooflike." A coin which has deeply reflective surfaces on both the obverse and reverse, resembling a Proof coin. Commonly pronounced as "dimple." Usually seen on Morgan dollars.
- **coin doctor**—anyone who alters the surface of a coin to "enhance its appearance" (by thumbing, artificial toning, whizzing, etc.), hoping to fetch a higher price.
- **CCE**—an online, dealer-to-dealer trading network for PCGS-, NGC-, ANACS-, and ICG-certified coins. Dealers post and trade sight-unseen and sight-seen bid/ask prices in real time on this electronic platform.
- **crackout**—an encapsulated coin that is thought by the owner to be of a higher grade than is on the holder. It is "cracked out" of the plastic holder and resubmitted with the hope of getting a higher grade.
- **fish**—a buyer or seller who is unaware of the true market value of a coin and buys or sells it at a price not commensurate with its worth.

- **fresh material**—coins or items that have not been on the numismatic market for many years.
- **flip**—a 2"×2" pliable plastic holder for a coin.
- **flip a coin**—selling a coin immediately after purchasing it, hopefully for a quick profit.
- **Godzilla**—an extremely attractive ("killer") coin.
- ***Greysheet***—a monthly publication providing current wholesale bid prices for problem-free, sight-seen numismatic coins.
- **hammer price**—the price at which the winning bidder wins the auction lot upon which he was bidding.
- **juice**—the commission paid on a coin at auction. The usual "juice" on a coin bought at a major auction is 10–25% over the hammer price.
- **junk Unc**—a Mint State coin worth only the bullion value. An Uncirculated 1964-D Washington quarter could be considered "junk Unc." Also a very low grade (MS-60) Uncirculated coin.
- **leave money on the table**—mistakenly sell something for a good deal less than its actual value.
- **lock 3**—a coin that would easily garner a MS-63 grade from a grading service. Can use any number corresponding to the estimated grade ("lock 2," "lock 4").
- **made coin**—the most recent grade on an encapsulated coin that has been submitted to a grading service more than once.
- **melt**—a coin worth only bullion value. Also the intrinsic value of a coin based solely on its bullion content.
- **newps**—new purchases.
- **P/L**—"Prooflike." A coin with especially reflective surfaces.
- **Pop**—"Population Report." Periodic publications issued by grading services. They indicate the number of coins that have been given a certain grade for each date and mintmark submitted. (Figures are generally considered less reliable due to resubmissions of the same coin, which skews the total.)
- **PQ**—"Premium Quality." When a certified coin is felt to be at the upper end of the grade on the holder. It may be called by the owner a "PQ" piece for the grade.
- **playing the game**—resubmitting a coin to one or more grading services several times, hoping it will come back with the (higher) grade you feel it is.
- **rip**—buying a higher-grade coin at a lower-grade price; purchasing a coin at a very attractive price.
- **roadrunner**—a dealer who works the shows but does not have a table. Sometimes also referred to as a "road warrior." See also "vest-pocket dealer."

- **score**—consummating a big-profit deal. Also referred to as a "hit."
- **sheet at**—"What does that coin 'sheet at?'" What is the price from the *Greysheet?*
- **shot coin**—a coin that one feels has a good chance of receiving a higher grade from a grading service than the grade currently assigned to the coin.
- **slab**—an encapsulated coin from one of the grading services.
- **Slab City**—any one of the third-party grading services.
- **thumbing**—a deceptive practice of trying to reduce the visibility of an abrasion on a coin (a light scuffmark on the cheek of a Morgan dollar, for example), by getting a bit of oil from the corner of one's nose on the thumb and carefully rubbing it into the affected area of the coin. This has a tendency to reduce the shiny appearance of the abrasion and possibly hide the distracting mark.
- **trap coin**—a coin that is priced at top dollar for the grade but barely, or does not, meet that grade. The buyer may get "trapped," as he could have difficulty reselling the piece.
- **vest-pocket dealer**—usually a small-volume dealer who has no table at a show and/or does not own a coin shop. See also "roadrunner."
- **white coin**—a coin with no toning whatsoever on it, just the original, "white" luster.
- **worked**—a coin that has been submitted to multiple third-party grading services in the hope of attaining a higher grade.

## Acronyms and Companies

Numismatics is also full of shorthand—acronyms and abbreviations that collectors and dealers use every day. This section decodes the most common ones so you can follow along without missing a beat, whether reading auction listings or chatting at a show.

- **ANA**—American Numismatic Association. A nonprofit educational organization that promotes the study and collection of coins and related items, serving collectors, the public, and academics. It is the world's largest organization for coin and paper money collectors, offering educational programs, resources, conventions like the World's Fair of Money, and publications. The ANA was founded in 1891 and received a US federal charter in 1912. For more information, visit money.org.
- **ANACS**— American Numismatic Association Certification Service. A coin-grading service that provides certification and grading for a variety of coins, tokens, and medals. It is America's oldest numismatic certification service, founded in 1972 by the ANA. ANACS authenticates and grades coins, encasing them in secure, tamper-evident holders, and providing

expert evaluation for value and authenticity. For more information, visit anacs.com.

- **ANS**—American Numismatic Society. An organization that studies coins, currency, medals, tokens, and related objects from all cultures and time periods. Headquartered in New York City (until a planned move to Toledo in 2028), it houses a vast research collection and library to support numismatic studies, education, and collecting. The ANS offers membership, publications, lectures, and access to its collection and resources for academic specialists, collectors, and the public. For more information, visit numismatics.org.
- **CAC**—Certified Acceptance Corporation. A third-party service that verifies the quality of coins already graded by services like PCGS and NGC. Coins that meet CAC's high standards for authenticity and quality receive a sticker on their original holder, with a green sticker for coins that are high-end for their grade and a gold sticker for coins that exceed the grade entirely. Recently, CAC has also launched its own full grading service, CAC Grading (CACG), which uses the same stringent standards but provides its own graded encapsulation. For more information, visit cacgrading.com.
- **ICG**—Independent Coin Grading Company. A professional third-party service that authenticates, grades, and encapsulates rare coins, tokens, and medals. It provides an objective assessment of a coin's condition to help with its value and authenticity. For more information, visit icgcoin.com.
- **NCBA**—National Coin & Bullion Association, formally known as the Industry Council for Tangible Assets (ICTA). A 501(c)(6) trade association for the rare coin, precious metals, and currency community. It serves as an industry watchdog, working to protect the interests of its members by promoting a favorable legislative and regulatory climate through lobbying, advocacy, and member education on compliance. The organization also provides resources and networking opportunities to its members. For more information, visit ncbassoc.org.
- **NGC**—Numismatic Guaranty Company (formerly known as Numismatic Guaranty Corporation of America). A leading third-party coin grading and authentication service for coins, tokens, and medals. Founded in 1987, NGC provides certification that includes grading, attribution, and encapsulation in secure holders. For more information, visit ngccoin.com.
- **NLG**—Numismatic Literary Guild. A nonprofit organization for authors, editors, writers, and other content producers who write about coins, medals, tokens, and other numismatic items. Founded in 1968, it hosts an annual awards competition to recognize excellence in numismatic literature and content and fosters a community for numismatic writers and publishers. For more information, visit nlgonline.org.
- **PCGS**—Professional Coin Grading Service. A company that provides third-party authentication and grading for rare coins, medals, and tokens.

Founded in 1985, PCGS uses a standardized system and expert numismatists to evaluate a coin's condition, authenticity, and other attributes, then encapsulates it in a tamper-evident holder. For more information, visit pcgs.com.

- **PNG**—Professional Numismatics Guild. A non-profit organization of top rare coin, paper money, and precious-metals dealers that is dedicated to upholding a high standard of ethics and professionalism in the numismatic industry. To become a member, dealers must meet strict requirements, including having a minimum of three years of experience, agreeing to a strict code of ethics, and submitting to a background check and binding arbitration for disputes. The PNG's mission is to protect collectors and investors by ensuring members adhere to principles of Knowledge, Integrity, and Responsibility. For more information, visit pngdealers.org.

# Recommended Reading for Collecting US Coins

The following is a curated list of recommended reference books on US coins. This selection can by no means remain exhaustive—new titles emerge regularly, and the field continues to evolve—but it provides an outstanding foundation and a deep well of knowledge for collectors at any level. The timeless axiom "buy the book before the coin" was first coined by prominent numismatic dealer and bookseller Aaron Feldman in the early 1970s and later popularized by Q. David Bowers. Knowledge remains the best defense against overpaying, fraud, or missing key details; arm yourself with information first. Most of these books are readily available through coin dealers, numismatic specialty retailers, online marketplaces, or major publishers like Whitman.

## General Guides and Starter Books

***A Guide Book of United States Coins*** (commonly known as the "*Red Book*") by R.S. Yeoman (edited by Kenneth Bressett and Jeff Garrett in later editions; Valuation Editor: Jeff Garrett)

Foundational "bible" of US numismatics, with pricing, mintages, history, grading basics, Mint data, colonials, commemoratives, and bullion. Essential for beginners; includes relative values and historical pricing.

***Handbook of United States Coins*** (companion to the *Red Book*; commonly known as the "*Blue Book*")

Focuses on dealer purchasing prices, for realistic selling values. Mirrors *Red Book* content but practical for market transactions. *Red Book* focuses on what you can expect to pay to buy a coin; *Blue Book* focuses on what you can expect to receive for selling a coin to a dealer.

***Cash in Your Coins: Selling the Rare Coins You've Inherited*** by Beth Deisher

Beginner-friendly for inherited collections; covers inventorying, basic grading, US coin types with color images, terminology, and dealing tips. Good to use in conjunction with the most recent edition of the *Blue Book*.

***United States Coinage: A Study by Type*** by Jeff Garrett and Ron Guth

Overview of US coin types, with color photos of finest-known examples. Helps identify collecting interests; includes virtual type set. Great for beginners and as a coffee-table book.

***America's Money, America's Story*** by Richard Doty

Broad history of US money from colonial times to the present, featuring items from the Smithsonian National Numismatic Collection.

## Grading Guides

***Official ANA Grading Standards for United States Coins*** (edited by Kenneth Bressett)

ANA standards, with photos, descriptions, and wear details for each US series from half cents to double eagles. Essential for condition assessment.

***Grading Coins by Photographs: An Action Guide for the Collector and Investor***

Visual tool with full-color photos of wear on key features and explanatory text.

**Coin World's *Making the Grade: Comprehensive Grading Guide for U.S. Coins***

Large format, with photos for grade/type, color maps, wear diagrams, and series descriptions.

## Varieties and Specialized References

***Cherrypickers' Guide to Rare Die Varieties of United States Coins*** by Bill Fivaz and J.T. Stanton (earlier editions)

Details rare varieties (doubled dies, overdates); a must-have for variety hunting.

***Walter Breen's Complete Encyclopedia of U.S. and Colonial Coins*** by Walter Breen

In-depth historical, design, mintage, variety, and error information from colonials to modern; all-in-one reference with photos and enlargements.

## Official Red Books Series (Specialized Guides by Q. David Bowers)

***A Guide Book of Lincoln Cents***

Expanded history, details, and varieties for Lincoln cents.

***A Guide Book of Morgan Silver Dollars***

In-depth on Morgan dollars.

## Additional Series Titles (examples from Whitman's 27+ Official Red Books)

***A Guide Book of Half Cents & Large Cents***

***A Guide Book of Buffalo and Jefferson Nickels***

***A Guide Book of U.S. Commemorative Coins***

## Series-specific Beyond the *Red Book*

*Mega Red Editions (Expanded* Red Books*)*

***Official Red Book Mega Red***

Denomination-focused expansions, with extra grading, pricing, and research.

## History, Hoards, and Notable Rarities

***100 Greatest U.S. Coins*** by Jeff Garrett and Ron Guth

Stories behind iconic rarities (e.g., 1913 Liberty nickel, 1804 dollar).

***American Coin Hoards and Treasures*** (also titled *American Coin Treasures and Hoards*) by Q. David Bowers

Narratives of discoveries, shipwrecks, and finds.

***Million Dollar Nickels*** by Mark Borchardt, Paul Montgomery, and Ray Knight

Detailed history of the 1913 Liberty nickel, including provenance, early collectors, and industry insights (focus on the Walton specimen).

***The History of the United States Mint and Its Coinage*** by David W. Lange

Mint origins, processes, branch mints, designers, and production history from the colonial era on.

***The History of United States Coinage as Illustrated by the Garrett Collection*** by Q. David Bowers

Study of early US collecting using the Garrett family collection.

## Comprehensive References and Almanacs

***Coin World Almanac***

700+ pages of indexed facts on coins, paper money, history, legislation, mints, bullion, and more.

***The MacMillan Encyclopedic Dictionary of Numismatics*** by Richard G. Doty

Alphabetical explanations of numismatic terms and items (e.g., chop marks, mules, scrip).

## Next-Step Reading

Once you've mastered the basics with the core references above, the following books from the broader numismatic literature offer rewarding depth for focused pursuits. These are not essential for beginners but become invaluable as you narrow your interests—whether to a single series, die varieties, errors, or early American issues. Seek current editions where possible; many are available used or through specialty dealers. Start with one or two books that match your growing passion.

*Series-Specific Deep Dives*

***The Complete Guide to Lincoln Cents*** by David W. Lange

Exhaustive guide on Wheat and Memorial issues; ideal once the *Red Book*'s Lincoln section whets your appetite.

***The Enigmatic Lincoln Cents of 1922*** by Tom DeLorey

This meticulously researched volume finally unravels one of the most enduring mysteries in 20th-century US coinage: the bizarre and dramatic variations seen on 1922 Lincoln cents struck at the Denver Mint.

***The Complete Guide to Buffalo Nickels*** by David W. Lange

Full attribution, date-by-date analysis, and variety checklists for this popular series.

***The Authoritative Reference on Morgan Dollars*** (commonly called the *VAM Book*) by Leroy C. Van Allen and A. George Mallis

The definitive die-variety catalog for Morgan dollars; a must for "VAM hunters."

*Variety & Error Classics*

***Cherrypickers' Guide to Rare Die Varieties*** by Bill Fivaz and J.T. Stanton (latest edition)

The updated standard (earlier editions already noted above).

***The RPM Book*** by John A. Wexler and Tom Miller

Comprehensive reference for repunched mintmarks—perfect if you discover an odd mintmark.

*Early US and Type Coin Masterworks*

***Penny Whimsy*** by William H. Sheldon

The foundational large-cent book; poetic, opinionated, and still relevant for 1793–1814 coppers.

***United States Early Half Dollar Die Varieties 1794–1836*** by Al C. Overton (latest update by Donald Parsley)

The "Overton number" bible for Bust halves.

*Investment and Market Perspective*

***High Profits from Rare Coin Investment*** by Q. David Bowers

Classic (if dated) market philosophy. Read critically for historical context, not current advice.

# Why Not Join a Specialty Club?

Journals and newsletters published by specialty clubs provide interesting articles, announcements about upcoming meetings, and other information.

## Ancient and Medieval Coins

Classical & Medieval Numismatic Society
    Website: www.cmns.ca
    Focuses on education and research in classical and medieval numismatics

## Books

Numismatic Bibliomania Society
    Website: www.coinbooks.org
    Publishes *The E-Sylum* weekly newsletter

## Checks

American Society of Check Collectors
    Website: asccinfo.com
    Publishes *The Check Collector* quarterly

## Credit Cards

American Credit Card Collectors Society
Website: www.creditcollectibles.com

## Elongated Coins

The Elongated Collectors
Website: www.tecnews.org
Participates in ANA conventions and produces *TEC News*

## Error Coins

Combined Organizations of Numismatic Error Collectors of America (CONECA)
Website: conecaonline.org
Focuses on errors and variety education

## Foreign Numismatics

American Israel Numismatic Association
Website: www.theshekel.org
Publishes *The Shekel*
Numismatic International
Website: numis.org
Promotes international coin collecting
Philippine Numismatic & Antiquarian Society
Website: www.pnas.ph
Promotes Philippine numismatics and antiquities
Polish American Numismatic Society
Website: pans-club.org

## Paper Money

International Bank Note Society
Website: www.theibns.org
Publishes *IBNS Journal*
Latin American Paper Money Society
Website: www.numismondo.net/lansa
Focuses on Latin American notes
Paper Money Collectors of Michigan
Facebook: facebook.com/groups/220258691093517
Emphasizes Michigan-related paper money
Society of Paper Money Collectors
Website: www.spmc.org
Publishes *Paper Money*

## Primitive Money

International Primitive Money Society
Facebook: facebook.com/internationalprimitivemoneysociety/

## Private and Pioneer Coins

Society of Private & Pioneer Numismatics
Website: pioneergold.wordpress.com
Publishes *The Brasher Bulletin*

## Silver Art Bars

International Association of Silver Art Collectors
Website: https://thesilverbugle.org
Active through ANA events; dedicated to silver rounds and rectangles

## Souvenir Cards

Souvenir Card Collectors Society
Website: https://www.souvenircards.org/
Active through ANA events; focuses on numismatic souvenir cards

## Tokens and Medals

American Medallic Sculpture Association
Website: amsamedals.org
Promotes American fine art medals
Casino Collectibles Association
Website: www.ccgtcc.com
Preserves gaming history
Love Token Society
Website: lovetokensociety.com
Collects engraved coins
Maryland Token & Medal Society
Website: www.mdtams.org
Publishes *Maryland TAMS Journal*
Michigan Token & Medal Society
Facebook: facebook.com/michtams1965
Promotes exonumia collecting
National Utah Token Society
Website: www.nationalutahtokensociety.org
Preserves Utah tokens and medals
Original Hobo Nickel Society
Website: www.hobonickels.org
Focuses on hand-carved nickels

Token & Medal Society
Website: www.tokenandmedal.org
Publishes *TAMS Journal*

## United States Coins

Barber Coin Collectors Society
Website: www.barbercoins.org
Studies Charles E. Barber designs
Bust Half Nut Club
Website: www.busthalfnutclub.org
Dedicated to early half dollars
Early American Coppers
Website: www.eacs.org
Focuses on colonial and early coppers
The Fly-In Club
Website: flyinclub.org
Studies James B. Longacre designs: Flying Eagle and Indian Head cents
John Reich Collectors Society
Website: www.jrcs.org
Focuses on early US silver and gold
Liberty Seated Collectors Club
Website: lsccweb.org
Focuses on Liberty Seated coinage
National Silver Dollar Roundtable
Facebook: facebook.com/Nationalsilverdollarroundtable
Promotes silver dollars
Society of Silver Dollar Collectors
Website: ssdcvams.com
Studies Morgan and Peace dollar varieties
Southern Gold Society
Website: southerngoldsociety.org
Studies Southern branch mints and private Southern minters

## Wooden Money

International Organization of Wooden Money Collectors
Website: www.woodenmoney.org
Publishes *Bunyan's Chips*

## Writers & Young Collectors

Numismatic Literary Guild
Website: nlgonline.org
Awards for numismatic writing

Young Numismatists of America
818 N. Cascade Ave.
Colorado Springs, CO 80903
Website: www.money.org/yn-america
Youth-led club

# 10 Rules of Thumb for Coin Collecting

1. Don't buy government-issue coins at the issue price from the Mint—you can almost always purchase them later at a lower price on the "after-market" from dealers.
2. Unless you know the dealer and that his grading is relatively accurate, don't buy coins from magazine or newspaper ads at cut-rate prices. Lower-than-average advertised prices usually mean over-graded coins.
3. A good way to get a "fix" on a low-ball advertiser is to check his prices on sets of coins (Proof, Mint, Prestige Sets, etc.) to see how they compare with the prices other (known, established) dealers are charging. If these prices are comparable while his other prices are quite low, beware!
4. Never buy coins from a telemarketer—or anything unsolicited over the phone.
5. All MS-63s (or 64s, 65s, etc.) *are not the same.* There is quality in every grade! Look for high-end, premium-quality coins in the particular grade you want, even if you have to pay a little more for them.
6. Join a coin club. If there's not one in your area, start one! There are many benefits in becoming an active member of a club, and you'll enjoy it, believe me!
7. Display bourse floor etiquette when attending a coin show. Be respectful and considerate of a dealer's time and space.
8. Attend the ANA Summer Seminar in Colorado Springs! Take advantage of a full week of wall-to-wall numismatics on just about any subject you want. Go once, and I'll guarantee you'll want to return year after year.
9. Learn to grade! Develop self-confidence using proper basic techniques so you'll be able to tell MS-63 from MS-64 from MS-65, etc. If you're buying encapsulated coins, as has been said over and over, "Buy the coin, not the slab."
10. Have fun!

# 25-Question Coin Quiz

Here are 25 questions based on all the previous text. I suggest that you quiz yourself on these, and for any you don't answer correctly, refer back to that chapter. The answers appear on page 122. (No peeking!)

1. Dave Bowers maintains that the key to making advantageous purchases in the coin market is one word: ________________________.
2. When holding a coin, you should always hold it with your ______________ and ______________ and hold it over a ______________.
3. The recommended magnification to use when grading a coin is ______________________________.
4. Wear is often signaled by a telltale _______________________ on the high points of the coin's surface.
5. You should avoid using plastic holders containing _________________ when storing your coins.
6. Always examine the third side of a coin, the ____________________.
7. When a coin is cleaned (dipped, etc.), the grading factor most affected is __________________________________.
8. It's a good idea to _______________________ your stored coins periodically to ensure they are not being affected by negative elements.
9. In coin parlance, what does "DMPL" mean? ____________________________________
10. What does "PQ" mean? _____________________________________
11. Where is the American Numismatic Association (ANA) headquartered? ________________________________
12. What do ANACS, CACG, ICG, NGC, and PCGS have in common? ____________________________________
13. The tooth-shaped design around the rims of some coins are called ____________________________________.

14. A specially minted coin, struck at least twice on specially prepared planchets by specially prepared dies, intended primarily for collectors is called a ______________________________.
15. A flat spot on the Buffalo's hip on the Buffalo nickel or on the right knee of Liberty on the Standing Liberty quarter, which can denote wear, is sometimes referred to as the ____________________ effect.
16. There is ________________ in every grade.
17. On any portrait coin, be certain to check the ______________ for ______________________________.
18. On the Walking Liberty half dollar, you may want to examine the ________________ on the obverse to confirm a loss of luster (wear) after seeing a difference in color on the eagle's _________________________ on the reverse.
19. What grade was once considered "The Grade of the Future"—and has become exactly that? ____________________________
20. When writing to a dealer, researcher, etc., requesting information, you should always enclose a ______________________________.
21. At an auction, you should always ________________________ and then stick to it.
22. One of the best kept secrets of the ANA is the annual ______________ __________ in Colorado Springs.
23. When mailing coins of any value, you should never send them via ___________________________
24. When attending a convention, never __________________________ without first asking permission.
25. As in any hobby, the main objective in numismatics is to ______________________________.

Turn page for answers.

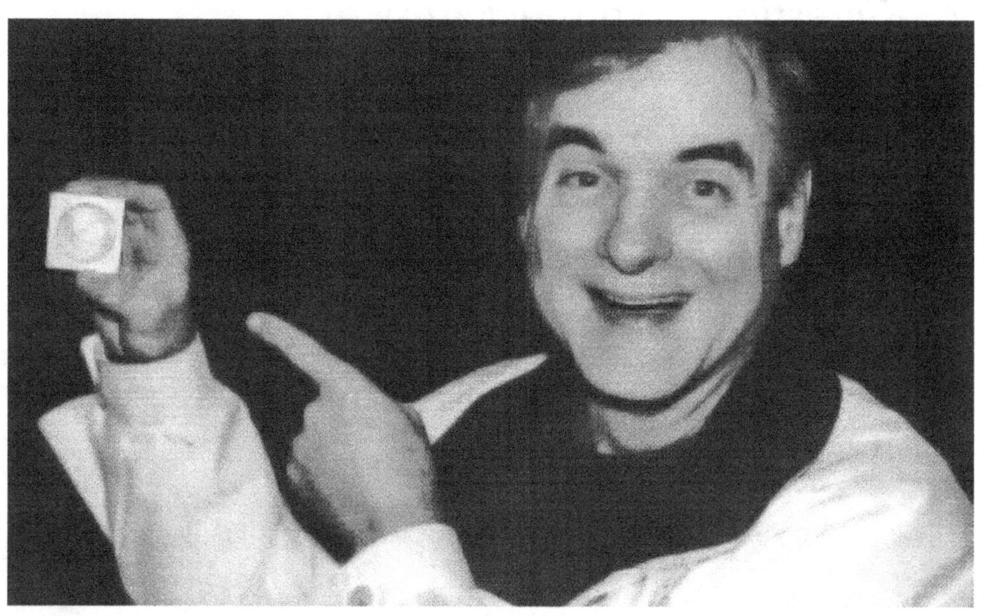

"WOW! LOOK WHAT I FOUND!" (Ron Wichman, Metropolitan Coin Club of Atlanta)
The knowledge gained in this book is a first step in your journey as a numismatist! With this information you are ready to embrace the community, history, and art that makes coin collecting such an exciting and fulfilling hobby. And who knows what gems you might find along the way?

# 25-Question Coin Quiz Answers

1. Knowledge
2. Thumb and index finger / soft surface
3. 5× to 7× power
4. Color difference
5. PVC (Polyvinyl chloride)
6. Edge
7. Luster
8. Check or examine
9. "Deep Mirror Prooflike"
10. "Premium Quality"
11. Colorado Springs, CO
12. They are all independent, third-party grading services who grade and encapsulate submitted coins
13. Denticles or dentils
14. Proof
15. Mesa (effect)
16. Quality
17. Cheek or face / hairlines or slide marks
18. Right field behind Liberty / neck feathers, breast
19. AU-58
20. Stamp or SASE (self-addressed stamped envelope)
21. Set a limit for how much you want to spend
22. Summer Seminar
23. Certified Mail
24. Reach into a dealer's case
25. Have fun!

# Index


**Air-Tite,** 10, 18
**albums,** 9, 10, 18, 55
**American Numismatic Association (ANA),** xvi, 16, 21, 26–27, 39, 103, 108 *(see also ANACS)*
  **Summer Seminar,** xvi, 117, 120, 122
  **World's Fair of Money,** xi, 103
**American Numismatic Association Certification Service (ANACS),** 15, 23, 101, 103–104, 119
**American Numismatic Society (ANS),** 104
**auction,** 13, 25, 29–31, 102, 120
**blank,** 92, 95
***Blue Book,*** 101, 107
**bourse,** 21–24, 95, 100–101, 117, 120
**Bowers, Q. David,** ix, xv, 3–4, 40, 107, 109, 110, 119
**branch mint,** xi, 47, 58, 82– 89, 91, 95, 109
**Bressett, Kenneth,** xv, 40, 107, 108
**Buffalo nickel,** xi, 46–48, 57, 59, 61, 73, 82, 97, 100, 108, 110, 120
**Bust half dime,** 73
**Bust half dollar,** 73
**CAC Grading (CACG),** 23, 27, 38, 104, 119 *(see also "Certified Acceptance Corporation (CAC)")*
**Campbell, Randy,** xv, 82
**capsule,** 10, 18, 119
**Certified Acceptance Corporation (CAC),** 19, 38, 104 *(see also "CAC Grading (CACG)")*
**cherrypicking,** 22, 23, 101, 108, 110
**Circulated,** 42, 72, 75, 93, 96
**cleaning,** xii, 8–9, 13–16, 99, 119
  **damage,** 13
  **methods,** 13–16
  **overdipping,** 8–9
  **PVC (green slime),** 16
**clubs,** xii, xiii, 3, 117
  **specialty,** 25, 111–115
***Coin World,*** xv, 3–4, 25–26, 108, 109
**CoinWeek,** 25
**commission,** 29, 30, 102
**contact marks,** 39–40, 44, 47–48, 53, 55, 58, 61–62, 67, 69, 72, 78
**convention,** 21–24, 120
**damage,** 8–9, 13, 33
  **contamination,** 19
  **fingerprints,** 5
  **humidity,** 11, 17
  **PVC (green slime),** 10, 14
  **scratches,** 9–10, 18, 39–40, 55
  **spots,** 6, 15, 48
**dealer,** 3, 26–27, 65, 75, 93, 103, 105, 107, 109, 117, 120
  **advertising,** 25–26, 117
  **bourse,** 21–24, 95, 100–101, 102, 103, 117, 122

**selling to,** 107
**Deep Mirror Prooflike,** 119, 122
**design,** 66, 91, 97
**changes,** 49, 59, 67
**portrait,** 42, 49–50, 55, 58, 59–60, 63, 65, 66, 67, 100, 120, 120
**die,** 91, 92–93, 97
**dipping,** 8–9, 14, 119 *(See also "overdipping")*
**doubled die,** 50–51, 55–56, 60, 65, 91, 93, 97, 100, 101
**eBay,** xiii, 25, 30
**edge,** 5–6, 19, 38, 92–93, 97, 98, 99, 119, 122
**encapsulation,** 10, 19, 30, 101, 103, 103–105, 117
**enjoyment,** 3–4, 27, 117, 120, 122
**error,** ix, xi, 7, 81, 91, 93, 100, 108, 109–110, 112
**etiquette,** 22–24, 26–27, 117
**examining,** 6–8, 38, 119, 122
**lighting,** 7–8, 38
**tip-n-turn method,** 8 *(see also "tip-n-turn")*
**eye appeal,** 37, 38, 39–40, 47–48, 53, 64, 69, 70, 72, 78
**First Class Mail,** 34–35
**flip,** xiii, 9, 17–18, 19, 102
**PVC-free,** 9, 10, 17–18, 119
**Franklin half dollar,** 63–64, 67, 82
**Full Bell lines,** 63
**Garrett, Jeff,** 107, 108, 109
**gold,** 87–89, 114
**grading,** 37–68, 44–45, 47–48, 69–80, 100, 107, 108, 117
**accuracy,** 76, 117
**AU,** xi, xii, 42, 47, 69–80, 120, 122
**bean sticker,** 19, 38, 104
**color designation,** 39–40, 41–42, 44
**description,** 39–40
**Mint State,** xii, 42, 53, 57–58
**quality,** 69, 72, 75–77, 117, 120
**GreatCollections,** 25, 30
***Greysheet,*** 30, 76–77, 84, 102, 103
**hairlines,** 9, 13, 39–40, 43, 52–53, 55, 60, 65, 122
**holding,** 5–7
**Independent Coin Grading Co. (ICG),** xvi, 23, 101, 104, 119
**Indian cent,** 41–43, 73, 81, 114
**investment,** 3, 110
**Jefferson nickel,** 49–51, 55, 65, 108
**Full Steps,** 50
**varieties,** 50–51
**Kennedy half dollar,** 65
**knowledge,** 31, 101, 122
**books,** xii, 3, 107–110
**importance of,** 3–4, 107
**Liberty Seated half dollar,** 73
**Lincoln cent,** 44–45, 59, 73, 81, 108, 109–110
**livestream,** 25, 29
**loupe,** xii, xiii, 6–7, 38, 67
**Hastings Triplet,** 7, 38
**luster,** 39–40, 41–42, 44–45, 47–48, 49, 53, 57–58, 60, 61–62, 66, 69, 72, 74, 75, 78, 96, 101, 103, 122
**magnification,** 6–8, 38, 39, 43, 44, 93, 119, 122
**mailing,** 25–27, 120, 122
**market value,** 30
**melt price,** 55, 59, 63–64, 102
**Mercury dime,** 52–54, 59, 73, 82, 97
**Full Bands,** 52–53
**mesa effect,** 46, 57, 120, 122
**Metropolitan Coin Club of Atlanta,** xii, xviii, 77
**Mint State,** xii, 15, 37, 40, 49, 51, 61–62, 64, 65, 75, 98, 102
**scale,** 39–40, 70, 78–80
**minting,** 91–93, 109
**mintmark,** 8, 47, 50, 56, 61, 62, 81, 88, 91, 98, 99, 100, 102, 110
**Morgan dollar,** ix, xv, 58, 66, 70, 73, 76, 78–80, 82–87, 96, 99, 108, 110, 114
**Deep Mirror Prooflike,** 87, 101
**Mylar,** 9, 17–18, 19
**National Coin & Bullion Association (NCBA),** 104
**Numismatic Guaranty Company (NGC),** xiii, 10, 16, 23, 27, 30, 101, 104, 119
***Numismatic News,*** 25–26
**overdate,** 91, 98

**overdipping,** 8, 53, 58, 62, 75
**overmintmark,** 98
**patina,** 13, 15 *(see also "toning")*
**Peace dollar,** xv, 67–68, 73, 76, 86–87, 114
**planchet,** 42, 81, 91, 92, 96, 98–99, 100, 120
**polishing,** xi, 8–9
**pricing,** 13, 49, 69, 70, 75
**Professional Coin Grading Service (PCGS),** xiii, 10, 16, 23, 27, 30, 40, 101, 104–105, 119
**Professional Numismatics Guild (PNG),** 16, 26–27, 105
**Proof,** 14, 48, 65, 92–93, 96, 99, 101, 117, 120, 122
**Prooflike,** 102
**purchasing,** 3, 25–27, 65
**PVC,** xi, 9, 10, 14, 16, 17, 19, 122
**quality,** 3
***Red Book,*** 99, 107, 108–109
**Registered mail,** 34, 35–36
**repunched date,** 99
**repunched mintmark,** 56, 60, 99, 100, 101, 110
**Roosevelt dime,** 55–56, 65
  **Full Bands,** 55
  **varieties,** 55–56
**shipping,** xii, 26, 30, 33–36
  **insurance,** 34–36
  **tracking,** 34, 35, 36
**slab** *(See "encapsulation")*
**Standing Liberty quarter,** ix, 57–58, 82, 97, 120
  **Full Head,** 57
**Stanton, J.T.,** xvi, 108, 110
**staples,** 18, 33
**storage,** xii, 9–12, 17–19, 119
  **environment,** 11–12, 17
  **home,** 11–12, 17
  **PVC-free,** xi, 19
  **safe-deposit box,** 11, 17
***The Numismatist,*** xii, 25–26
**third-party grading,** xv, 13, 19, 30, 78–80, 100–101, 102, 103, 104, 122
  **encapsulation,** 10, 19, 30, 96, 101, 103, 104-105, 117
**tip-n-turn,** 8, 38, 43, 44, 49, 52, 55, 96
**toning,** 53, 57, 61, 64, 101, 103
**Uncirculated,** 15, 37, 41, 59, 75, 77, 99
**USPS,** 34–36
**varieties,** ix, xi, 7, 21–23, 50–51, 55–56, 60, 65, 81, 88, 91, 92, 93, 100, 101, 108, 109, 110
**Walking Liberty half dollar,** 59, 61–62, 75, 82, 120
**Washington quarter,** 59–60, 73, 82
  **varieties,** 60
**weak strike,** xv, xvi, 42, 47, 54, 58, 61, 63, 66, 68, 81–89
**wear,** 42, 44, 46–47, 49–50, 52, 55, 57–58, 59–60, 61, 63, 65, 66, 67, 70, 74, 81, 119
**Weinberg, Fred,** xvi, 87
**Whitman,** 9, 21, 107

# About the Authors

## Bill Fivaz

Bill Fivaz has been passionately collecting coins since 1950 and is recognized as one of America's foremost authorities on grading, die varieties, and Mint errors. A lifelong student and teacher of numismatics, Bill has instructed grading classes at the ANA Summer Seminar for over 25 years, delivered the Educational Forum at the FUN Convention for over 30+ years, and served as a longtime consultant to ANACS.

His contributions to the hobby have been widely honored: he is a recipient of the ANA Farran Zerbe Memorial Award (1995), two ANA Medals of Merit (1984 and 1989), ANA Numismatist of the Year (2001), ANA Hall of Fame (2002), and the Numismatic Ambassador Award (1982). A former ANA board member and prolific exhibitor with numerous Best-in-Show awards, Bill is also co-author of the best-selling *Cherrypickers' Guide to Rare Die Varieties* and authored two *Counterfeit Detection Guides,* one covering most counterfeit coins encountered and one specifically on gold counterfeits. He has also co-authored the "Mint Errors" section of *A Guide Book of United States Coins* (the *Red Book*) from 1980 to 2018 and has published countless articles and educational slide programs.

A Life Member of the ANA (No. 1100) and dozens of regional and specialty organizations, Bill specializes in Buffalo nickels, Mercury dimes, Morgan and Peace dollars, Mint errors and varieties, hobo nickels, love tokens, and US commemoratives.

Born in Fulton, New York, in 1934, Bill is a 1956 graduate of Hamilton College. After serving in the US Naval Reserve, he enjoyed a 36-year sales career with Nestlé Co. before retiring to devote even more time to the hobby he loves. He and his late wife, Marilyn, (married 1956) have two children, Bill (deceased) and Diane; two grandchildren, Jacob and Erin; and two great-grandchildren, Ella and Jaxson.

## David C. Crenshaw

David Crenshaw's lifelong love affair with coins began in childhood with Whitman blue folders and quickly evolved into a passion for error coins and die varieties—a direction forever cemented the first time he did business with Bill Fivaz by mail at age fifteen in 1973 and later when he finally met Bill in person at the 1977 ANA World's Fair of Money in Atlanta.

A graduate of the Atlanta numismatic scene, David spent years dealing error coins (under the memorable catalog banner of "Nobody's Perfect"), worked at Rare Coins of Georgia, served as Director of Numismatic Research for Whitman Publishing, managed the Whitman Coin & Collectibles Expo for nearly a decade, and chaired the highly successful 2006 ANA National Money Show in Atlanta.

Since 2013 he has guided the National Coin & Bullion Association, first as the chief operating officer and since 2021 as executive director, while helping launch initiatives such as the Concerned Collectors Coalition and a revitalized association website.

Widely honored for his service to the hobby, David is the recipient of the ANA Medal of Merit (2024), PNG Significant Contribution Award (2025), FUN Numismatic Ambassador Award (2019), multiple ANA Presidential and exhibitor awards, and has been named to *Coin World*'s "100 Most Influential People in Numismatics" list numerous times.

An accomplished speaker, award-winning exhibitor, and frequent contributor to club and regional publications, David remains as enthusiastic about coins today as he was filling those first blue folders. He and his wife Kathy are proud empty-nesters who enjoy time with daughters Carrie and Katy; son-in-law Casey; grandchildren Payton, Ashlyne, and Colton; and their rescued terrier mix, Coco.

www.ingramcontent.com/pod-product-compliance
Lightning Source LLC
LaVergne TN
LVHW020634100826
845148LV00012B/2180

* 9 7 9 8 2 1 8 9 1 8 6 7 5 *